THE ROYAL HORTICULTURAL SOCIETY
PRACTICAL GUIDES

BULBS

THE ROYAL HORTICULTURAL SOCIETY
PRACTICAL GUIDES

BULBS

ROD LEEDS

A Dorling Kindersley Book

LONDON, NEW YORK, MUNICH, MELBOURNE, DELHI

SERIES EDITOR Annelise Evans
SERIES ART EDITOR Ursula Dawson
DTP DESIGNERS Louise Paddick, Louise Waller
PRODUCTION MANAGER Sarah Coltman

MANAGING EDITOR Anna Kruger
MANAGING ART EDITOR Lee Griffiths

Produced for Dorling Kindersley by

studio cactus ©

13 SOUTHGATE STREET WINCHESTER HAMPSHIRE SO23 9DZ

SENIOR EDITOR Jane Baldock
SENIOR DESIGNER Sharon Moore

First published in Great Britain in 2001
Reprinted 2003
by Dorling Kindersley Limited,
80 Strand, London WC2R 0RL

A Penguin Company

02 03 04 05 10 9 8 7 6 5 4 3

Copyright © 2001 Dorling Kindersley Limited

A CIP catalogue record for this book is available from the British Library

ISBN 0 7513 4723X

Reproduced by Colourscan, Singapore
Printed and bound by Star Standard Industries PTE Ltd, Singapore

See our complete catalogue at

www.dk.com

CONTENTS

USING BULBS IN THE GARDEN 7

An introduction to using bulbs for year-round colour. How to choose bulbs for cut flowers or dried seedheads. Using bulbs to provide fragrance, colour, and structure in the garden.

PLANTING PLANS FOR BULBS 33

A SPRING BORDER 34
A SUMMER BORDER 36
AN AUTUMN BORDER 38
A WINTER BORDER 40
A LAYERED BORDER 42
BULBS IN FORMAL BEDS 44
BULBS IN CONTAINERS 46

LOOKING AFTER YOUR BULBS 49

Buying healthy bulbs, preparing the soil and planting, routine care and maintenance, how to store bulbs, forcing prepared bulbs, growing your own bulbs, and avoiding problems.

CHOICE BULBS FOR THE GARDEN 65

A photographic guide to a selection of some of the best garden bulbs, including information on hardiness, moisture requirements, and flowering times.

Index 78
Acknowledgments 80

USING BULBS IN THE GARDEN

WHAT ARE BULBS?

BULB IS A GENERAL TERM used by gardeners for plants with a food-storage organ that allows them to grow and flower quickly once the optimum conditions occur. They may be true bulbs, such as daffodils and lilies; corms, such as crocuses; tubers, such as cyclamens and dahlias; or rhizomes, such as wood anemones. These "bulbs" have all evolved for different reasons, and have different flowering and resting periods.

SEASONAL CHOICES

For the gardener, evolution has provided a huge and colourful array of bulbs for every season of the year. Many of these are fully hardy, but some, such as cannas, are half-hardy and are grown in the same way as seasonal bedding plants. In cooler climates, frost-tender plants need to be cultivated in a frost-free greenhouse or conservatory.

Fortunately, many bulbous plants can be grown easily in temperate climates, if the gardener considers the planting position and site to his or her advantage.

Each bulb is a highly condensed plant; its embryonic roots, stem, leaves, and flower are all contained within it, just waiting for the appropriate moisture and temperature conditions for growth to begin.

AUTUMN COLOUR *Cyclamen hederifolium is an attractive autumn-flowering cyclamen that is particularly effective when it is planted in large groups or drifts.*

◀ RUBY TULIPS *Planted in solid blocks of colour, tulips and grape hyacinths make a strong impact.*

BULBS FOR ALL SEASONS

VERY VERSATILE AND EASILY GROWN PLANTS, bulbs can provide colour from some of the most graceful of garden flowers throughout the year. Traditionally we think of the highlights produced by bulbs such as daffodils in spring and the stately tulips that follow, but there are many more bulbs to consider. The vast range of bulbs available provides flowers from across the colour spectrum for every month of the year.

SPRING

This is the one season when even non-gardeners view with appreciation the bulb's efforts to drive away the winter blues.

It is possible to have daffodils flowering in the garden for over two months. The season starts with selections such as *Narcissus* 'February Gold' in early spring. The beautiful white 'Thalia' follows in mid-spring and the sweetly scented double white 'Cheerfulness' a little later. One of the last daffodils to flower is 'Tripartite', which has several golden yellow flowers per stem and often looks its best in late spring.

Tulips provide some of the most vibrant flower shades, with hues ranging from yellow through orange to red and violet. White tulips can be used to tone down and give welcome contrast to the brighter flowers. The medium and shorter varieties are less inclined to bend in inclement weather and tulips such as *T.* 'Purissima' and *T.* 'White Triumphator' stand proudly over smaller spring flowers.

The choice of other bulbs in spring is enormous. There are the small Reticulate irises, with such a great colour range, and the pure blue of the scillas and glory of the snow (*Chionodoxa*), which soon carpet the ground through their seed production. Widening the range can be achieved by growing the little South American *Ipheion uniflorum* 'Wisley Blue', a pale blue, starry flower that rises above its leaves. Other colours are becoming available for this plant. A similar effect can be achieved by growing *Anemone blanda*, often blue, but also available in white, purple, and red.

NODDING NARCISSI
The small-flowered Narcissus *'Jack Snipe' and* Anemone blanda *have a grace and beauty that is never overbearing.*

SPRING BULBS

Chionodoxa forbesii
Ipheion uniflorum (all)
Narcissus 'Dove Wings'
Narcissus 'Irene Copeland'
Narcissus 'Jack Snipe'
Narcissus 'Jetfire'
Narcissus 'Minnow'
Narcissus 'Mount Hood'
Scilla siberica 'Spring Beauty'
Tulipa linifolia Batalinii Group
Tulipa praestans 'Fusilier'

RIOT OF RED
The bright flowers of Anemone pavonina *are show stoppers in the spring. They thrive in the sunniest and driest spot in the garden.*

SUMMER

With the arrival of summer there are, ideally, no bare patches of soil: either the gardener has planted a tapestry of species or nature has done the same. For bulbs to make an impact at this time of year they must be tall and well able to fend for themselves in the jungle of foliage. This dense summer cover can, however, often be useful since some taller bulb foliage becomes rather ragged by summer and is best hidden by surrounding plants. Alliums, camassias, and galtonias fall into this category, but their globes and spires add interest to any border, although they work particularly well when grown in conjunction with herbaceous plants.

The tender bulbs can now be planted out or left in their pots to decorate patios or pathways. Bulbs such as cannas, gladioli, and dahlias are very colourful and can create dramatic effects. Lilies begin to rise in the borders at this time of year, showing off their attractive stems and leaves. The hybrid lilies are often the easiest to grow, but they lack some of the beauty of the species. Often referred to as the giant lily, *Cardiocrinum giganteum* loves a rich, damp situation, when its stems – bearing heart-shaped leaves and scented trumpet flowers – may reach heights of up to 2m (6ft) to form a spectacular sight.

ARTFUL ALLIUMS
The pompon-headed alliums are excellent garden plants. Purple here, but also available in white, these bulbs make marvellous infilling between herbaceous flowers in late spring.

SUMMER BULBS

Allium giganteum
Allium 'Globemaster'
Camassia cusickii
  'Zwanenburg'
Camassia leichtlinii
  'Semiplena'
Galtonia candicans
Lilium 'Karen North'
Lilium 'Marie North'
Lilium martagon var. *album*

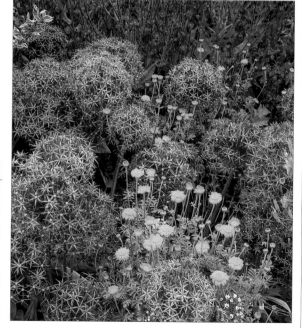

AUTUMN

Many autumn bulbs produce flowers on naked stems, their leaves developing in the following spring. When they are planted (in late summer, earlier than spring bulbs), the space that will be taken by their leaves the following year has to be considered, for some – like the colchicums and amaryllis – have abundant and far-reaching foliage. Nerines and amaryllis lead the way. Both flower profusely if planted under a sunny wall, with the bulb tops just visible. They have pink, and occasionally white, trumpet-shaped flowers held on stout stems.

The ivy-leaved cyclamen, *Cyclamen hederifolium*, is superb when grown in drifts since its mixed white and pink flowers are soon followed by beautiful green and silver patterned leaves. Providing a complete contrast in colour are the sternbergias, with bright yellow goblet-shaped flowers. Lovers of hot, sunny spots, they bloom over a long period, with some lingering into midwinter.

Often wrongly referred to as "autumn crocuses" are the colchicums, which are in the same family as daffodils (*Narcissus*) and usually pink, a colour never achieved by a true crocus. Colchicums look very effective when grown in groups in quite wide borders, planted to allow enough space for their leaves to develop in spring.

Closely planted autumn bulbs brighten up a tired garden after the summer

Colchicum speciosum 'Album' is a crystalline white goblet above a lime green stem – a perfect combination with a good constitution able to resist the vagaries of the autumn weather. Last to be admired here is a real autumn crocus, *Crocus speciosus* 'Oxonian', a rich dark purple flower that is very tolerant of planting position.

ALTERNATIVE FOR AUTUMN
Planted deeply, these South African bulbs, Eucomis bicolor, *are reliable late summer and autumn flowerers. They also make ideal container plants.*

AUTUMN BULBS

Amaryllis belladonna
Colchicum byzantinum
Colchicum speciosum
  'Album'
Colchicum 'Waterlily'
Crocus speciosus 'Oxonian'
Dahlia (all)
Lilium speciosum
Nerine bowdenii
Sternbergia lutea

WINTER BULBS

Cyclamen coum (all)
Eranthis hyemalis
Galanthus elwesii
Galanthus nivalis
  (all)
Hippeastrum (all)
Hyacinthus orientalis
  (all)
Leucojum vernum
Narcissus 'Paper White'

▲ SPLASH OF PINK
*Colchicums are easy and
effective flowers to grow for
prolonging interest in autumn
borders, either as an edging,
or as infilling between plants.*

▶ A WINTER BORDER
Cyclamen coum *with all its
colours and leaf markings
makes a very interesting bed
in winter. It is easy in every
respect and deserves to be
more widely grown.*

WINTER

At this time of year, the cultivation of bulbs for indoor decoration is very popular. Traditionally, prepared hyacinths and daffodils (*Narcissus*) have long been the stalwarts for brightening up the season, but gaining a larger share of the market are the hippeastrums: large-flowered hybrids that can be planted in autumn to flower in the depths of winter.

In the bleak outdoors it is possible to have bulbs in flower right through the winter, cheering all who pass their carpets of colour. It is best to plan these winter plantings along the sides of pathways for ease of access. If the bed can be raised, so much the better, for any scents can then be appreciated. The snowdrop (*Galanthus*) is an amazing little bulb, tough, easily grown,

and with different varieties that can be in flower from mid-autumn through to early spring. The common snowdrop (*Galanthus nivalis*) is a great survivor and is found naturalized in many parts of the UK. Find a supplier who sells these bulbs "in the green", which means they have been damp-packed and are available to buy as flowering finishes. The survival rate of these bulbs is far greater than if you plant dry bulbs bought in summer.

Equally impressive in winter are the winter aconites (*Eranthis*), little yellow flowers surrounded by ruffs of leaves, which break through the soil at the first sign of warmth. The winter-flowering cyclamen, *Cyclamen coum*, is marvellous as an impact plant, and its magenta to white flowers are impervious to the cold.

BULBS FOR PICKING

Picked flowers show off the marvellous intricacies of their markings and scent so that they can be fully appreciated. Even if you are not a flower arranger, a simple slim vase is perfectly adequate, even for a single bloom. Some flowers do not open fully outside if the temperature or light intensity are low. This is particularly relevant during the winter months when both of these problems can be overcome easily in the warmth of a house.

CUT FLOWER SELECTION

The amazing arrangements seen at flower shows give an idea of the types of bulb that can be grown for picking. If you pick regularly, it is best to grow the bulbs exclusively for this purpose as part of the vegetable garden. Bulbs, such as gladioli, are excellent as cut flowers but are hard to place in an informal garden, so if you plant them in rows between the onions and carrots you can crop them with the vegetables.

CUTTING AND KEEPING FLOWERS

When selecting stems for cutting, pick those in loose bud and take only the length you need, leaving as many leaves as possible so that the bulb can be built up for the following year. Once picked, cut the stem at an acute angle so that it can draw up as much water as possible and thereby remain fresh longer. Put the flowers in a cool place in deep water, and remove any leaves that might be completely underwater to prevent them from rotting. Use one of the brands of proprietary flower crystals to prolong the life of the stem, or add a teaspoon of sugar and a dash of bleach for the same effect.

The water in cut flower arrangements should be replaced every week to help keep it fresh-smelling, and dying flowerheads need to be removed to keep the arrangement looking attractive for longer.

> Smaller bulbs can be used to make exquisite individual arrangements

Many bulbs – including amaryllis, nerines, and lilies – are excellent in arrangements being both long-lasting and having rigid stems. Note that lily pollen can stain clothing so be aware of this both when planting up lily borders and when arranging cut lilies. It is preferable to retain the stamens, if possible, as they provide such a contrasting feature.

ELEGANT ANEMONES
Anemones make long-lasting cut flowers. Here they are tied tightly, making an unusual and eye-catching arrangement.

Tulips are excellent as cut flowers and hold themselves well. Cut the stems as long as possible with the flowers in bud and they will always open.

Make sure you cut the stem below the point at which the leaves are attached

always a pleasure. During the less-abundant times of the year, and particularly in midwinter, it is often a challenge for the gardener to collect flowers. The search can be surprisingly rewarding, however, especially if the frost has not been too severe, as still to be found are sternbergias, crocuses, snowdrops (*Galanthus*), and cyclamens, while forced daffodil (*Narcissus*) and hyacinth blooms can also be included.

Flowers collected for a midwinter arrangement can be surrounded by evergreens and other winter flowers in a simple arrangement set in a shallow bowl.

SEASONAL ARRANGEMENTS

An old custom of collecting flowers and foliage for a particular event was revived early on in the 20th century by the great gardeners Vita Sackville-West and Lady Scott. This simple arrangement is called a tussie-mussie and has its origins as a form of nosegay that was used to disguise unpleasant odours. Today, luckily, this purpose is rarely necessary, but the collection of flowers for an occasion is

DAFFODIL "TREE"
A stunning use of daffodils. These flowers have short cups (coronas) and make ideal subjects for a tight ball arrangement.

BULBS FOR FLORISTRY

Allium cristophii
Allium hollandicum
Crocosmia × *crocosmiiflora* 'Dusky Maiden'
Crocosmia × *crocosmiiflora* 'Star of the East'
Dahlia (all)
Gladiolus Grandiflorus Group
Leucojum aestivum 'Gravetye Giant'
Lilium (all)
Narcissus (all)
Nerine bowdenii
Tulipa (all)

BULBS WITH DECORATIVE SEEDHEADS

THE MORE BULBS YOU GROW, the more you will find that they leave an attractive legacy at the end of the summer, namely the dry seedhead, which is also full of seed. The most familiar seedhead is that of the allium, which is spherical and designed to break off the stem and be blown around arid plains, shedding seeds as it goes. Most of the seedheads that naturally become rigid with age do so as an adaptation for seed dispersal, usually by wind.

DRYING BULB SEEDHEADS

The damp conditions of autumn begin the process of decay, leaving the gardener the choice of picking and drying, or leaving the seedheads in situ. The time for harvesting seedheads depends upon the dryness of the head, which is always best pulled after a dry, sunny day. Once harvested, the stems need to be hung in a dry, airy place for a few weeks so that they can continue to dry and shed their seeds. One method is to place the seedheads in large paper (not plastic) bags, so that, as the seeds are

> The seedheads of the pompon onions are ideal for drying

released from the chambers, they will be collected in the bag and will be ready to sow. When you remove the seeds, look out for insects that will have emerged from the seed capsules as they dried.

SUITABLE BULBS

The pompon alliums – including *Allium atropurpureum, A. hollandicum, A. rosenbachianum, and A. schubertii,* – are ideal for preserving as dried flowerheads, and each differs in height and structure, something you notice only at close quarters. If the heads are not collected, they look very beautiful covered in hoar frost during the winter and often remain well into the following spring before they finally snap and collapse. An unusual way to display seedheads like *Allium hollandicum* 'Purple Sensation' is to plant long drifts of them through the border. Attractive in summer, they have pompon seedheads in autumn.

The taller fritillaries, tulips, and some lilies form larger capsules that contain flat, lighter seed, which drifts away in the breeze

GARDEN GLOBES
The old flowerheads of alliums make effective dried spherical globes for an everlasting display.

When dried, the seeds may become trapped in the capsules of the flowerhead once the seed case opens. These capsules can also be harvested as soon as the leaves turn brown and can be dried in the same way as alliums. You may, however, need to strip off any remaining leaves attached to the stems before displaying the seedheads.

The most imposing of all bulbous seedheads is seen on the stem of the giant lily, *Cardiocrinum giganteum*, from Asia. Its large, hollow stem is stout and tall, and after the precious seeds have been collected, it can be placed in a container to dry. Cardiocrinum seed capsules are large and have three sides, each edged with teeth that look rather like those found on a Venus flytrap. The teeth hold on to the seeds until the wind is strong enough for there to be a reasonable chance of distant seed dispersal. Dried cardiocrinum seedheads are so strong and durable that the hardest task in preserving them is deciding how best to keep them free of dust.

SEEDHEAD CHOICES

Allium cristophii
Allium 'Globemaster'
Allium hollandicum
Allium hollandicum
 'Purple Sensation'
Allium nigrum
Allium schubertii
Fritillaria (all species)
Tulips (all)

FRITILLARIA
SEEDHEADS

Dried seedheads are very long-lasting and can be used either in mixed dried-flower arrangements, or within fresh arrangements provided that the stems do not reach the water (or they will begin to rot). Alternatively, dried seedheads can also be coloured with spray paint, for festival decorations or for children's creations.

GONE TO SEED
Some seedheads, such as this cardiocrinum, can be left to dry in the open garden until such time as they are required for use in dried decorations. These dried capsules and the hollow stem are very substantial and can be up to 2m (6ft) tall when eased from the ground.

BULBS FOR FOLIAGE

THE LEAVES OF BULBS are often regarded as their greatest drawback, taking weeks to die down and looking unsightly as they yellow with age. Daffodils are the most reviled in this respect, so much so that trials have been conducted to see how soon their leaves could be removed without affecting subsequent flowering. Other bulbs, however, produce leaves that provide additional interest, giving dramatic structure and colour to borders.

LEAVING THE LEAVES

Bulb leaves fall into three categories: those, such as daffodils, that need hiding or just ignoring; those, such as crocuses and corydalis, which are so fleeting once the sun becomes stronger in spring that they soon wither and virtually disappear; and, luckily, a third group with attractive foliage that is pleasing in its own right. Of the latter, some have leaves that complement the flowers, while others – usually autumn-flowering bulbs – make their leaf growth the following spring. Whenever the leaves develop, do not be tempted to remove them until they begin to turn yellow, when their job is finished. In the case of daffodils, it is recommended that you leave the leaves for six weeks and do not tie or knot them.

Architectural leaves can make a stunning impact before flowering occurs

---

The combination of leaves and flowers in some bulbs is worth considering. Dog's-tooth violets (*Erythronium*) have broad, often mottled leaves that emerge prior to flowering. All cyclamens have attractive leaves, particularly the autumn-flowering species *C. hederifolium* which has silver and green foliage that remains for over eight months. Tulips are rarely thought of as foliage plants, but some have leaves with wavy margins, others are mottled, and a few have truly variegated leaves. The dahlia

'Bishop of Llandaff' has a very dramatic growth of black-red foliage before the bright red blooms appear.

Other bulbs produce much taller leaves that are either rigid structures, as in the crocosmias and gladioli, or have a symmetrical arrangement along the stem, as seen in some lilies and fritillaries. The planting of these taller bulbs adds dramatic structure to a border, but you do need to consider their ultimate height.

BLADES OF GREEN
The sword-like leaves of the hybrid crocosmias are very attractive and last well into autumn.

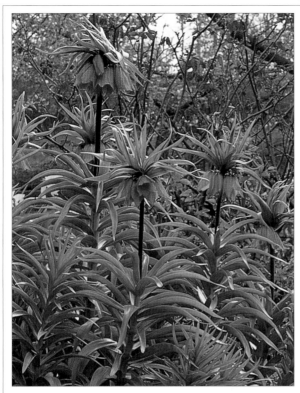

FOLIAGE BULBS

Canna (all)
Cardiocrinum giganteum
Erythronium californicum
Erythronium dens-canis
Erythronium revolutum
Fritillaria imperialis (all)
Iris bucharica
Lilium martagon
Lilium speciosum
Lilium superbum
Tulipa kaufmanniana Group
Tulipa kolpakowskiana
Tulipa praestans 'Unicum'
  (has variegated leaves)

◄ SPIKY GREEN LEAVES
There is a special lushness given to the border by the stately habit of the Crown Imperial fritillaries.

▼ LEAFY COMBINATION
Bulbs often have very attractive and variable foliage that provides a complementary foil for their flowers.

Cannas, although tender, have large paddle-shaped leaves on a scale befitting their size, and look good as a centrepiece to seasonal bedding or in large containers. Better planted in large numbers are lilies, whose architectural leaves make an impact in the middle of a border, before the flowers open.

Finally, to the spring foliage of autumn-flowering bulbs. Some gardeners complain of the exuberant extent of the leaves but strong leaf growth means prolific flowering later. So enjoy the glossy leaves of the colchicums, nerines, and amaryllis throughout mid- and late spring. It is only in early summer that the leaves look unsightly, and by then other plants mask the decay. Colchicums are adaptable and can be planted among shrubs as long as some sun reaches them each day. Nerines and amaryllis need a sunny site, and must not be hidden or they will fail to flower.

BULBS IN CONTAINERS

PLANTING BULBS IN CONTAINERS is an ideal way for gardeners with only a small amount of space to have permanent colour just where it is needed and best appreciated. When they are not flowering, pots can simply be placed out of sight and the bulbs allowed to grow on. Areas as small as window boxes can be utilized very successfully in this way as long as the bulbs can be removed with their roots intact so that they can be grown on in a reserve bed.

CONTAINER CHOICE

An amazing array of containers can be brought into use as homes for plants. One requisite for bulbs is that they must have an adequate depth: approximately two or three times the bulb's own depth in planting and then at least that depth again for root development. Also, water must be able to drain away quickly; if it cannot, the situation can soon be remedied by drilling extra holes in the base of the container.

Bear in mind that plastic pots are lighter than terracotta – an important consideration if you wish to move them – and their weight can be further restricted by using a layer of polystyrene pieces as drainage in the base of the pot. Plastic pots can be placed inside more decorative pots for display. The combined thickness of the two pots slows down evaporation by keeping the soil cooler, thereby reducing the need to water. Use soil-based compost such as John Innes No. 3, so that the bulbs will build up after flowering for the following year.

When the bulbs have flowered and are placed back in the garden, do continue to water them and feed them with a dilute tomato-type fertilizer until the leaves begin to die down in order to aid the following year's bulb growth. If space is limited, the pots of resting bulbs can be stacked up until it's time to check the bulbs and start their growth again.

▲ HEIGHT AND STRUCTURE
Tulips provide the focal point for the display in this container, creating height and bringing colour to the arrangement.

◀ FANCY FRITILLARY
Planting combinations of bulbs in containers provides pleasing colour and shape. Here the highlight is Fritillaria pallidiflora.

FLOWERS THROUGH THE YEAR

Container gardens can challenge the grower who wants to have bulbs in flower for every day of the year. In the early part of the year, crocuses, glory of the snow (*Chionodoxa*), grape hyacinths (*Muscari*), and snowdrops (*Galanthus*) will take you well into spring, when ipheions and small daffodils (*Narcissus*) come into their own. In summer, the amazing multiflora begonias give a very long-lasting display. The small hardy onions, such as golden garlic (*Allium moly*) and nodding onion (*A. cernuum*), look lovely alongside the white flowers of *Ornithogalum nutans* and the star of Bethlehem (*O. umbellatum*). If space allows, consider any type of lily as they look good in containers, they do not take up too much space, and they make a stunning backdrop to any display.

All cyclamens – including the slightly tender florists' cyclamens – make excellent container plants, and although they are slow-growing, they will flower while young. They are best suited to semi-shaded positions and can last for many decades if repotted occasionally.

The small-flowered dahlias are hard to beat for the density of their flowers, which last from summer through to autumn; regular deadheading will encourage them to flower for longer.

Plastic pots can be placed inside more decorative pots for display

---

A microclimate against a wall or in an alley is surprisingly useful for protecting pots from extremes of temperature. During the winter, the common snowdrop (*Galanthus nivalis*) cultivars, *Iris reticulata*, *Crocus tommasinianus*, and *Cyclamen coum* soon bring colour to the dullest day.

BULBS FOR POTS

Colchicum tenorei
Crocus tommasinianus
  f. *albus*
Crocus tommasinianus
  'Ruby Giant'
Cyclamen coum
Dahlia 'Fascination'
Dahlia 'Preston Park'
Galanthus nivalis
  (all)
Hyacinthus orientalis
  (all)
Iris 'Harmony'
Iris 'Katharine Hodgkin'
Nerine undulata

POTTED DAHLIAS
Late in the season, dahlias can be placed against a background of foliage to enliven a border.

BULB CONTAINERS IN BORDERS

A USEFUL METHOD FOR MAKING A BORDER PERFORM CONSISTENTLY throughout the year is to introduce bulbs, by way of containers, to spaces that would otherwise lack interest once the first flush of spring has passed. This means of bringing instant colour to an area can be achieved simply by placing or burying containers in the border at a chosen spot. The use of such pots will, however, need careful consideration as to their colour, size, and stability.

FILLING SEASONAL GAPS

To make a feature of these container bulbs, quite large pots will be required, especially for bigger species. The moveable bulb pots need not be attractive if they are to be buried, so plastic is quite adequate. The plants will need a nursery in which to spend most of the year, where they are watered and fed ready for their big moment. Alternatively, some gardeners grow the bulbs in lattice pond baskets, sunk in the ground, and then move them to the required location (*see p.53*). This is a useful method for spring-flowering bulbs, which tend to be shorter, and has the advantage of leaving the roots free to grow once they extend beyond the basket, thereby reducing the need for watering.

SUITING BULBS TO CONTAINERS

Your chosen bulbs should be planted up in a good-quality soil-based compost such as John Innes No. 3. Container cultivation allows you the opportunity to grow any bulb you like by carefully matching the type of compost to the requirements of the bulb. Most bulbous plants prefer soil that is neutral or alkaline, but there are a few – often the woodlanders, for example, some lilies and their relatives – that prefer acidic conditions. *Lilium speciosum* and the American turkscap lily (*L. superbum*) require lime-free, ericaceous composts if they are to grow well. This compost dries out more quickly than the soil-based type and the bulbs will need liquid feeding throughout the growing season.

POTS OF BEGONIAS
Regular watering and feeding can keep these buried containers of begonias flowering for longer than those grown in the open border.

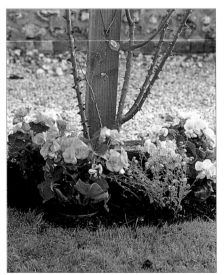

GOOD GAP FILLERS

Camassia cusickii
Camassia leichtlinii
Canna 'Assaut'
Canna 'President'
Canna 'Wyoming'
Eucomis bicolor
Gladiolus (all)
Lilium speciosum var. *rubrum*
Lilium superbum
Tulipa (all)

◀ LILIES IN A BORDER
These are among the best subjects for burying in a border. Lilies can be grown specially and staked before being planted out in a summer border.

▼ SURFACE CONTAINER
Tulips are ideally suited to growing in containers and bring a short term, but very welcome, burst of colour to the border in spring.

CHOICE OF CONTAINER

If you use plastic containers, make sure that they are free of deep folds or creases since such indentations can attract slugs and snails, which, in turn, may devour the bulb foliage and ruin all your careful preparation. An old bucket, especially a smooth-sided metal one makes an excellent subterranean planter. Drill holes in the base of the bucket for drainage.

> Tall plants in containers will benefit from some support

Whatever the container, if the plants are tall it is good practice to insert discreet supports before the bulbs grow and need staking. In borders, the taller the bulb, the greater the impact especially in summer when the perennial plants will be at their maximum height. White-flowered bulbs, such as galtonias and some lilies, look stunning against a background of dark, shady foliage. Red and orange bulbs are set off very well against grey foliage plants.

Pots of taller bulbs need to be anchored to the ground as wind can wreck a display. Heavy wire bent into hooks, with one end pushed well into the ground, is an effective anchor and can easily be hidden. Another option is to use large stones as top-dressing. A group of containers can be lashed together, or linked by stout wire bent to resemble paper-clips.

The last consideration is moving large, moist pots. Lifting is risky, so a sack barrow (like a porter's trolley) is essential for safe movement through the garden.

USING BULBS FOR FRAGRANCE

THE SCENT FROM FLOWERS – including bulbs – is one of their main attractions, and can be delightful on a still day at any time of the year. In winter, scent is harder to detect, as either the flowers do not release their perfumes so readily or the atmosphere inhibits their upward movement. If the individual flowers of some snowdrops (*Galanthus*) are picked and brought into a warm room, however, then the differing scents of the cultivars can be detected.

GARDEN SCENT

The use of raised beds as a method of bulb and small plant cultivation is known to be effective for many reasons. The fact that the flowers are nearer to the admirer is one, because this proximity brings their fragrance closer, which is particularly useful as many sweetly scented bulbs are quite small. Even without a raised bed, it is a good idea to consider planting scented bulbs close to doors and along pathways, where their perfumes can be regularly enjoyed.

Some of the bulbs native to the UK are very fragrant – a bluebell wood in mid-spring, for example, is full of the flowers' wonderfully sweet smell. In contrast, ramsons (*Allium ursinum*) can fill a damp wood with a pungent garlic odour, especially if the leaves are crushed. Most scents are far more subtle, and it is not

Bringing bulbous flowers into the home releases their fragrances

until you take home a bunch of flowers that you realize some have a special fragrance; indeed, the scent of jonquils (*Narcissus jonquilla*) can be quite overpowering in a confined space.

LILY FRAGRANCE
Lilies are renowned for their fragrance. Do be careful of the pollen when close to the flowers, as it can stain clothing.

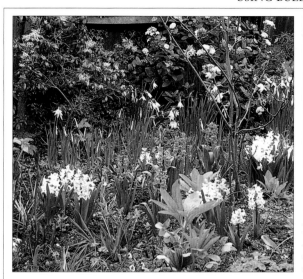

HEADY HYACINTHS
In the border the scent from
hyacinths is particularly
noticeable on a warm day.

Bulb scents are not very well documented so you may want to keep scent notes of your own. When your bulbs are in flower for the first time, try to place the smell. It may not always be a pleasant one. Some bulbs, such as the fritillaries, have a chemical smell like household bleach, while the crown imperial (*Fritillaria imperialis*) emits a foxy scent when either its leaves are crushed or its bulb damaged.

During warm, still, summer evenings daytime scents will mingle with those released at night. The perfumes of other plants, such as honeysuckle (*Lonicera*) and night-scented stocks (*Matthiola*), are joined at these times by that of the little cream *Gladiolus tristis*, which, like the others, attempts to attract moths as pollinators.

FRAGRANT BULBS INDOORS

Having bulbous flowers in the house or conservatory, either as cut flowers or grown in pots, brings their fragrances into a confined space for all to enjoy. Hyacinths,

for example, have a heady perfume that will fill a room for days. As cut stems, the range of scents from bulbs is much greater than expected. The grape hyacinths (*Muscari*) are very refreshing, tulips can be quite spicy, and many cyclamens are very sweetly scented. Experiment by picking different flowers; those from the winter months may well surprise you by their unexpected release of perfume in the warmer atmosphere, often undetected when the flowers bloom outside.

SCENTED DAFFODILS
Some daffodils, such as Narcissus *'Pipit', have*
a lovely, delicate scent. This is a bonus worth
checking when you are buying new bulbs.

NATURALIZING BULBS

To SEE BULBS NATURALIZED in grassland or light woodland is one of the most breathtaking sights. It does not need to be on a grand scale, but the effect can be copied in miniature around any deciduous tree. Wherever your site, you should be able to find a small space for such a planting, but do look first at nearby gardens and woods to see what thrives locally and start with these bulbs. When your bulbs start to spread, you will know that they are doing well.

PREPARATION

Naturalizing bulbs needs some preparation to ensure success. First, any tap-rooted plants like dandelions need to be removed from the area you intend to use and the grass cut prior to planting in autumn. If you are planting a small area then the flowering heights of your selected bulbs require sorting so that the smaller species are not smothered by, for example, lax daffodil (*Narcissus*) foliage. Normally, however, random planting looks the most natural, and to achieve this some people advocate gently throwing the bulbs into the site and then planting them where they fall. A bulb planter, which resembles a large pastry cutter, is useful, although for large-scale planting insert a spade and wiggle it back and forth to make a slit for the bulb. Refirm the hole with your boot (*see p.51*).

In woodland settings, which can mean a single deciduous tree but usually refers to a shady place where grass does not thrive, any grass that is present will have to be removed before planting. You are restricted to shade-loving woodland bulbs, which flower before the tree canopy fills out.

BULB CHOICE

Next comes the pleasant task of choosing your bulbs. A selection of native species has a very restful and quiet charm, and could consist of the Lent lily (*Narcissus pseudonarcissus*), snake's head fritillary

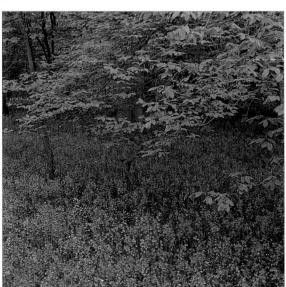

BLUEBELL CARPET
A bluebell wood in spring is a magnificent sight and, en masse, emits an attractive scent. Many of these sites are now protected by law from any disturbance.

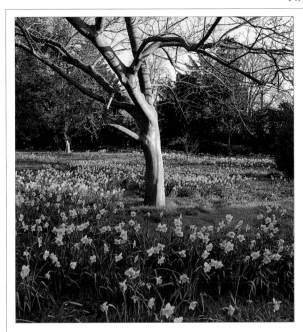

NATURAL SETTING

GRASSLAND

Colchicum (all species)
Fritillaria meleagris
Galanthus (all species)
Leucojum aestivum
Leucojum vernum
Narcissus (all)
Ornithogalum
  (all species)

WOODLAND

Anemone nemorosa
Cyclamen coum
Cyclamen hederifolium
Galanthus
  (all species)
Hyacinthoides hispanica
Hyacinthoides non-scripta
Lilium (all)
Muscari (all species)
Scilla (all species)

▲ DAFFODIL WOOD
Daffodils look their best in light woodland and open meadows, where they mimic the habits of nature.

▶ SPRING MEADOW
A mixed planting of different bulbs looks beautiful in spring. The grass can be cut in summer without damaging the bulbs.

(*Fritillaria meleagris*), common snowdrop (*Galanthus nivalis*), and an orchid such as the green-winged orchid (*Orchis morio*). For more colour, introduce scillas, tulips, crocuses, ornithogalums, winter aconites (*Eranthis*), and snowflakes (*Leucojum*). For autumn naturalization, good bulbs to try are *Colchicum autumnale*, the autumn crocus (*Crocus nudiflorus*), *C. ochroleucus*, *C speciosus*, and *C. medius*, all of which will thrive in short grass.

In the woodland garden there is an opportunity to experiment with many of the shade-loving bulbs from around the world, but do remember that it is not appropriate to naturalize exotic bulbs in native woodland unless it is an extension of your garden. Lilies thrive in a large space and look very natural. Selections have been made from the little wood anemone (*Anemone nemorosa*) so that a range of darker shades is now available, and even double selections can be planted to decorate the woodland floor.

Many of the scillas and grape hyacinths (*Muscari*) will also look very natural in woodland settings, and are best grown in large drifts to create a stunning effect. The colony will soon spread by self-sowing and will begin to appear completely wild.

BULBS FOR COLOUR

THE USE OF COLOUR in the garden needs to be planned and its effects understood. Using colours from opposing segments of the colour wheel will produce the most dramatic effects. Choosing colours from adjacent segments will produce more subtle combinations. Walk around local parks or public gardens for your initial inspiration for planting.

COLOUR WHEEL

USING HOT COLOURS

Hot colours are those at the red end of the spectrum. They are intense and vibrant, and seem to shorten the border by appearing to be closer to you than they really are. The use of bulbs with bold and lance-shaped leaves can mute the effect of hot colours and add to the "tropical" feeling. Such a border is usually best suited to a sunny position and is generally planted alongside herbaceous plants, where the bulbs soon provide height and dramatic colour. The bulbs are best planted in solid blocks of colour rather than separated out as individual bright spots.

The hot colours are found mainly in late spring- and summer-flowering bulbs, which in turn are usually medium to tall in stature. Tulips, crocosmias, cannas, and some anemones can all provide an eye-catching display. In warmer climates where sunlight is harsher, strong, fiery colours seem less strident; conversely, cool pastel shades appear washed out in bright sun but look vibrant in gardens that are situated in cooler climates. Try different plantings if the colours prove to be too much or are not to your liking. In an emergency, bulbs can even be moved in any season, and although they may not flower the following year, they will certainly survive.

SUNNY YELLOWS
A block of a strong colour, such as yellow, needs careful consideration, but can produce a stunning effect.

FIERY BULBS

Anemone × *fulgens*	*Dahlia* 'Doris Day'
Anemone pavonina	*Dahlia* 'Murillo'
Canna 'Assaut'	*Lilium pomponium*
Canna 'King Midas'	*Lilium pumilium*
Crocosmia × *crocosmiiflora* 'Emily Mckenzie'	*Tulipa* 'Apeldoorn'
	Tulipa 'Apeldoorn's Elite'
Crocosmia × *crocosmiiflora* 'Star of the East'	*Tulipa linifolia*
	Tulipa 'Orange Bouquet'
Crocosmia latifolia 'Lucifer'	*Tulipa praestans* 'Fusilier'
Dahlia 'Bishop of Llandaff'	*Tulipa* 'Red Riding Hood'

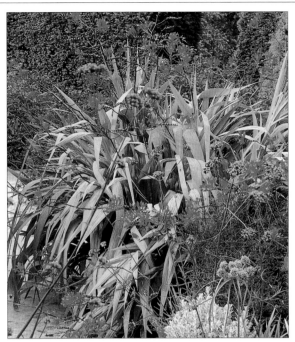

◀ RED AND PINK
The strong reds of crocosmias can be muted by the planting of an appropriate pink shade, such as that of the verbena, shown here.

▼ A TAPESTRY OF ORANGE
When planning a pattern of colours such as this one, always make sure that the flowering periods of the different bulbs are going to coincide.

Using Cool Colours

The English garden is renowned for its use of cool colours, which suit the climate and light intensity very well. Working with nature, bulbs can be used to enhance a border or an arrangement of patio containers for all four seasons. Here, white, pale blue, pink, and even pale primrose can make a very restful and beautiful display.

In winter, bulbs often reign supreme in providing early colour, when the snowdrop (*Galanthus*) and the white and pale pink forms of *Cyclamen coum* create a very cool

---

Cooler colours are best suited to regions with a lower light intensity

---

background during the shortest days of the year. As spring develops, the choice becomes immense, from the white and pale forms of scillas, grape hyacinths (*Muscari*), dog's-tooth violets (*Erythronium*), crocuses, daffodils (*Narcissus*), and puschkinias. These bulbs are best when interspersed with other plants such as lungwort (*Pulmonaria*) and Christmas roses (*Helleborus niger*),

and small shrubs such as *Daphne mezereum* f. *alba*. For pale primrose, *Fritillaria pallidiflora* has large pendent bells surrounded by beautiful leaves. The white snakeshead fritillary, a UK native, is one of the most beautiful bulbs when seen scattered throughout a spring planting.

During summer, the garden can be a refreshing place, especially on hot days, when the illusion of coolness is very welcome. At this time, the border will benefit from a mixture of herbaceous plants used as a backdrop for the transient bulbs. Holding its own with any plant is the giant lily (*Cardiocrinum giganteum*), with stout stems to more than 2m (6ft), topped by large, fragrant, trumpet-shaped flowers.

Taking up very little space are any of the white-flowered pompon alliums, with their leafless stems topped by a cluster of white flowers. Other, usually medium to tall, bulbs suitable for a summer planting are ornithogalums, camassias, galtonias, snowflakes (*Leucojum*), and lilies.

There are many famous white gardens that always look their best in summer. New planting ideas are tried and tested regularly in these gardens, so take a look

MUSCARI BLUES
Grape hyacinth bulbs need planting very close together to obtain this dense highlight to the spring border. There are abundant leaves which, later, make excellent weed-suppressing ground cover.

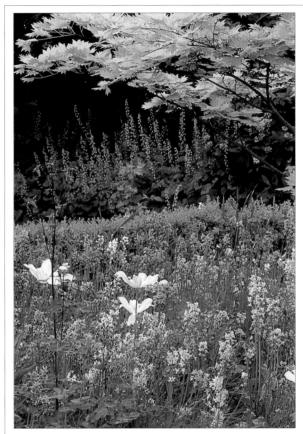

COOL BULBS

Allium 'Mount Everest'
Camassia cusickii
Crocus sieberi 'Albus'
Cyclamen hederifolium
  f. *albiflorum*
Galanthus plicatus
Galtonia candicans
Narcissus 'Thalia'
Ornithogalum narbonense
Ornithogalum nutans
Tulipa 'Purissima'

◄ COOL AND FRESH
By mixing colours, in this
case pink and blue bluebells,
a tapestry of pastel shades is
used to highlight the fresh
green leaves of a maple tree.

▼ BLUE SHADES OF AUTUMN
A true autumn crocus,
Crocus speciosus *'Oxonian',*
flowers without leaves and is
quite able to thrive in either
sun or light shade.

at some of them for inspiration. Emulate the schemes you find appealing, for very little is really new and there is no patent to a design or combination of plants.

In autumn, the light – slanting, and often hazy – is one of the attractions of the darkening year, so the planting of cool bulbs needs to reflect the muted tones of yellowing and decay. Try one of the most attractive and graceful bulbs of the year, *Colchicum speciosum* 'Album', a thick milky-white goblet-shaped flower on a lime-green stem. Like most autumn colchicums, it flowers without leaves, which do not begin to grow until the following spring. Another classic autumn plant is the white, and hardy, form of the usually pink *Cyclamen hederifolium*.

FORM AND STRUCTURE

BULBS BRING RELIABLE and regular form to borders and containers. Shrubs and trees may take time to mature and produce the desired effects. Bulbs, however, flower in the season following purchase and never increase in height as the years pass by. They may spread naturally, but to combat this, if it is not a characteristic you want to encourage, you face only the relatively easy task of lifting and replanting as many as you require during the resting period.

SEASONAL STRUCTURE

In contrast to the relatively short stature of winter and early spring bulbs, the species that flower later in the year are often taller and show greater diversity of colour and flower shape. The leaves of the later bulbs often have a most attractive shape, texture, and colour. For months after their flower stems have coiled and seed has been set, the two cyclamens, *Cyclamen coum* and *C. hederifolium*, have attractive foliage that can become so dense over the years that it precludes weeds and forms a substantial ground cover. The cyclamens' leaf colour varies from plain green to green with silver markings, plain silver, or pewter. Tempting as it may be to have weeks of flowers in autumn followed by more in winter and spring, do not plant these two species together, as *C. hederifolium* will overwhelm *C. coum* with its luxuriant leaves.

> Bulbous plants provide strong vertical lines within a border

The fresh leaves of most of the dog's-tooth violets (*Erythronium*) are beautifully mottled with silver or chocolate brown, similar to those of some Greigii tulips, such

STRUCTURAL ALLIUMS
Alliums are unique in that they provide these spheres of colour in the summer border and later architectural shape in the autumn. They love a sunny aspect and are sturdy plants that never need staking.

STATELY CANNAS
*Strong shape and colour
is provided by cannas.
Although tender, they grow
very quickly in spring to
provide an attractive centrepiece to a summer border.*

STRUCTURE BULBS

*Allium cristophii
Allium hollandicum
Cardiocrinum giganteum
Crocosmia* (all)
*Fritillaria imperialis
Lilium martagon
Lilium superbum*

as 'Red Riding Hood'. When thinking of foliage, consider the shape, clusters, and sheen of fresh leaves as these characteristics all add an extra dimension to plants we usually consider simply for their flowers. Equally, remember that flower stems are quite bare and may form strong vertical features in the garden long after the flowers have faded. Alliums, some fritillaries, and the giant cardiocrinum lily are all attractive in this respect.

The impact of the display in its entirety should also be considered at the time of planting. The ultimate height and spread need to be established, as well as the visual impact of the garden in other seasons. The shape created by the planting scheme may be thin and winding or a wide plot of densely planted bulbs designed to make a focal point of colour. Large bulbs, such as cannas, lilies, and fritillaries are bold enough in their own right to be used as individual plants in a mixed border, flowering and then quickly becoming submerged by summer foliage.

The popularity of formal structure provided by a tightly clipped box hedge is on the increase. This planting is usually in some form of geometrical pattern within which bulbs are planted to give blocks of contrasting colour or height and shape. The size of hedge needs to be considered when planting short bulbs such as muscari, hyacinths, and narcissus (*see p.44–45*).

PLANTING PLANS FOR BULBS

CHOOSING A PLANTING STYLE

THE VERSATILITY OF BULBS means that they can give new gardens an air of maturity within a single year, whilst in more established gardens they provide an almost instant fillip of colour or shape where it is needed. The plans shown here not only cover the traditional use of bulbs in spring, but also give further ideas for summer- and autumn-flowering bulbs, often rather neglected. Whatever your choice of season, bulbs can create the desired impact of colour or design.

CHANGES IN GARDEN DESIGN

Gardening trends are constantly evolving. The introduction of new bulbs and the development of micro-propagation has given the gardener a far greater choice at an affordable price. For instance, a few years ago, a single bulb of the beautiful spring *Crocus sieberi* 'Albus' was prohibitively expensive. Now it is so modestly priced that it is available in most plant retail outlets. For the avant-garde, the major flower shows create great excitement with their innovative ideas on design and planting. Bulbs often play their part, being used as architectural features and in specific colour blocks and bands to lead the eye through a display. The amateur gardener can copy elements of these ideas and incorporate them into most garden situations, and the new plants can be acquired as they inevitably become more readily available.

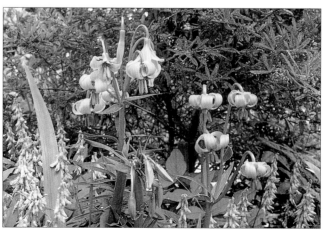

VIBRANT COLOUR
The orange-yellow lily (Lilium pyrenaicum) and the herbaceous pea (Lathyrus aureus) contrast with the dense blue flowers of the shrubby evergreen ceanothus. The lily and the pea are grown on the shady side of the shrub so that their colourful display lasts longer and is not bleached by the sun.

◀ ALLIUM STARS *Mixed alliums are attractively set off by the purple foliage of heucheras.*

A Spring Border

A border planted to be at its peak in spring is one of the highlights of the garden. Here, the traditional bulbs have been interspersed with mostly shrubby plants, which will add to the show and provide some year-round interest. Herbaceous plants, such as hostas and grasses, can be planted to provide cover for any bare patches of earth that are left behind once the bulb foliage begins to turn yellow and die down later in the season.

Fritillaria meleagris is one of the best, easiest to grow, and most subtly attractive of the fritillaries. It is available in purple or white.

Chimonanthus praecox, wintersweet, is a deciduous, arching shrub with stiff spikes of highy fragrant primrose flowers in spring.

Erythronium 'Pagoda' is a reliable hybrid with a number of backward-curving, yellow flowers on each stem and attractive, paddle-shaped leaves.

Phormium tenax provides evergreen spear-like leaves in green, purple, cream, and pink.

Fritillaria persica 'Adiyaman' is one of the few taller bulbs for spring with small, plum-coloured flowers up the stem.

Helleborus × hybridus is an evergreen plant. It gives a solid background to any border.

Pulmonaria 'Lewis Palmer' has attractive, ground-hugging leaves, often marbled with silver, and pink, blue, or white flowers.

Chionodoxa luciliae, glory of the snow, has bright blue and pink starry flowers.

Tulipa 'Queen of Night' has a beautiful dark plum-purple cup of petals. Bulbs can survive for many years without being lifted.

Ornithogalum nutans, star of Bethlehem, is an easy bulb for any situation that takes care of itself. It makes an attractive white feature.

Crocus chrysanthus 'Blue Pearl' reliably produces pale blue goblets that open widely in sunshine.

Sorbus reducta is a small suckering rowan with berries.

Muscari azureum is a bright blue spire that never fails, whatever the weather.

PLANTING PLAN

1 *Helleborus × hybridus*, 45cm (18in) tall
2 *Pulmonaria* 'Lewis Palmer', 35cm (14in) tall
3 *Phormium tenax*, 4m (12ft) tall
4 *Tulipa* 'Queen of Night', 60cm (24in) tall
5 *Fritillaria meleagris*, 30cm (12in) tall
6 *Fritillaria persica* 'Adiyaman', 1.5m (5ft) tall
7 *Chimonanthus praecox*, 4m (12ft) tall
8 *Erythronium* 'Pagoda', 15–35cm (6–14in) tall
9 *Sarcococca confusa*, 2m (6ft) tall
10 *Narcissus* 'Thalia', 35cm (14in) tall
11 *Chionodoxa luciliae*, 15cm (6in) tall
12 *Ornithogalum nutans*, 20–60cm (8–24in) tall
13 *Crocus chrysanthus* 'Blue Pearl', 7cm (3in) tall
14 *Sorbus reducta*, 1–1.5m (3–5ft) tall
15 *Galanthus plicatus* subsp. *byzantinus*, 20cm (8in) tall
16 *Tulipa praestans* 'Fusilier', 30cm (12in) tall
17 *Iris reticulata* 'J.S. Dijt', 10–15cm (4–6in) tall
18 *Oxalis adenophylla*, 10cm (4in) tall
19 *Iris* 'Harmony', 10–15cm (4–6in) tall
20 *Muscari azureum*, 10cm (4in) tall
21 *Daphne alpina*, 60cm (24in) tall
22 *Erythronium dens-canis*, 10–15cm (4–6in) tall

4m (12ft)

6m (20ft)

MORE CHOICES

TALL (over 90cm/36in)
Fritillaria imperialis

MEDIUM
(30–90cm/12–36in)
Narcissus 'February Gold'
Narcissus 'Jetfire'
Tulipa 'Queen of Sheba'

SMALL
(below 30cm/12in)
Muscari latifolium
Narcissus 'Jack Snipe'
Scilla bifolia

Sarcococca confusa is a small evergreen bush with scented flowers.

Narcissus 'Thalia' is a pale beauty of excellent stature and garden worthiness that will give years of pleasure.

Iris reticulata 'J.S. Dijt' is very reliable for cold areas. It has purple flowers in early spring.

Oxalis adenophylla is a tiny South American plant, which is not at all invasive. It is best-suited to a sunny site.

Tulipa praestans 'Fusilier' is a stunning Asian beauty with a number of very bright red flowers per stem.

Daphne alpina is a deciduous shrub that has scented, white flowers.

Galanthus plicatus subsp. *byzantinus* is a fine, broad-leaved snowdrop, which grows well in sun or shade.

Iris 'Harmony', although early into flower, will withstand the worst of any weather and continue to bloom.

ERYTHRONIUM DENS-CANIS
This is the only European member of this genus. The leaves alone make very attractive ground cover.

A SUMMER BORDER

This summer border is one in which bulbs predominate but have the support of other herbaceous and woody plants to provide the interest in the bed at other times of the year. The dark background of a yew hedge helps to set off the display. Summer bulbs are often tall and slim, taking little horizontal space, and this enables the gardener with a small space to grow an interesting range while avoiding undue overcrowding.

Ceratostigma willmottianum is a shrub that is stunning in autumn with masses of blue flowers. Late into growth, it is good for disguising bulb foliage.

Allium hollandicum is a tall drumstick onion which, in the form 'Purple Sensation', is a very impressive, dark purple.

Euonymus fortunei is an excellent and easy-to-grow evergreen shrub that can be pruned to the height and size required.

Daphne bholua gives winter interest to this area but is a slim shrub with shiny, attractive, pointed leaves in summer.

Crinum × powellii is a bold plant with arching leaves and pink trumpet flowers produced over a long period in summer.

Genista lydia is a light, arching shrub that flowers in late spring. It allows the tall bulbs to push through to flower.

Salvia patens is a herbaceous perennial with flowers freely produced and ideal for planting mid-border.

Allium moly is an excellent choice for the edge of the border. It revels in full sun.

ALLIUM CRISTOPHII
This is a very easy and reliable drumstick onion, with light purple flowers. New plants are freely produced by seed dispersal.

Allium cernuum, or the nodding onion, has clusters of bright purple-red bells and narrow foliage.

PLANTING PLAN

1 *Crinum* × *powellii*, up to 1.5m (5ft) tall
2 *Genista lydia*, 60cm (24in) tall
3 *Galtonia candicans*, 1–1.2m (3–4ft) tall
4 *Allium hollandicum*, 1m (3ft) tall
5 *Euonymus fortunei*, 60cm (24in) tall
6 *Daphne bholua*, 2–4m (6–12ft) tall
7 *Cardiocrinum giganteum*, 1.5–4m (5–12ft) tall
8 *Camassia cusickii*, 60–80cm (24–32in) tall
9 *Allium moly*, 15–25cm (6–10in) tall
10 *Salvia patens*, 45–60cm (18–24in) tall
11 *Ceratostigma willmottianum*, 1m (3ft) tall
12 *Allium cristophii*, 30–60cm (12–24in) tall
13 *Crocosmia* × *crocosmiiflora* 'Dusky Maiden',
   60–90cm (24–36in) tall
14 *Allium cernuum*, 30–60cm (12–24in) tall
15 *Callistephus chinensis* Milady Mixed,
   30cm (12in) tall
16 *Sedum spectabile*, 5–60cm (2–24in) tall
17 *Taxus baccata*, 10–20m (30–70ft) tall

3m (10ft)

3m (10ft)

MORE CHOICES

TALL (over 90cm/36in)
Crocosmia 'Lucifer'
Lilium martagon
Lilium regale

MEDIUM
(30–90cm/12–36in)
Gladiolus communis subsp.
   byzantinus
Lilium 'Red Night'
Ornithogalum pyrenaicum

SMALL (below 30cm/12in)
Allium insubricum
Allium oreophilum

Cardiocrinum giganteum
is the most dramatic of all summer-flowering bulbs. Grow a number together so that at least one or two are in flower each year.

Taxus baccata, or yew, hedges make an excellent backdrop to any border and are very easily controlled to suit the height and width requirements of the display.

Camassia cusickii can be accommodated throughout the border, and will propagate itself by seed dispersal.

Galtonia candicans is often called the summer hyacinth. This graceful, white-flowered bulb flowers for a considerable period.

Crocosmia × **crocosmiiflora 'Dusky Maiden'** has beautiful, dark foliage and orange flowers, and is quite hardy. It tends to be shorter in full sun.

Callistephus chinensis Milady Mixed, China aster, is a short-growing annual with double, Aster-like flowers in a range of colours. It is tolerant of drought.

Sedum spectabile is a late summer-flowering perennial with attractive leaves and large, flat flowerheads that attract bees.

AN AUTUMN BORDER

An attractive, almost unexpected, bonus of the autumn bulb border is the introduction of fresh flowers it brings to the waning summer garden. Small spring- and summer-flowering shrubs can be planted with the bulbs to bring foliage interest to the border in late autumn. A number of bulbs have attractive spring foliage, especially the cyclamen, with its silver-veined, ivy-shaped leaves which provide dense ground cover for many months.

PLANTING PLAN

1 *Amaryllis belladonna*, 60cm (24in) tall
2 *Crocus speciosus* 'Oxonian', 10–15cm (4–6in) tall
3 *Colchicum speciosum* 'Album', 18cm (7in) tall
4 *Festuca glauca*, 30cm (12in) tall
5 *Perovskia* 'Blue Spire', 1.2m (4ft) tall
6 *Sternbergia lutea*, 15cm (6in) tall
7 *Colchicum* 'Waterlily', 12cm (5in) tall
8 *Cyclamen hederifolium*, 10–13cm (4–5in) tall
9 *Eucomis bicolor*, 30–60cm (12–24in) tall
10 *Nerine bowdenii*, 45cm (18in) tall

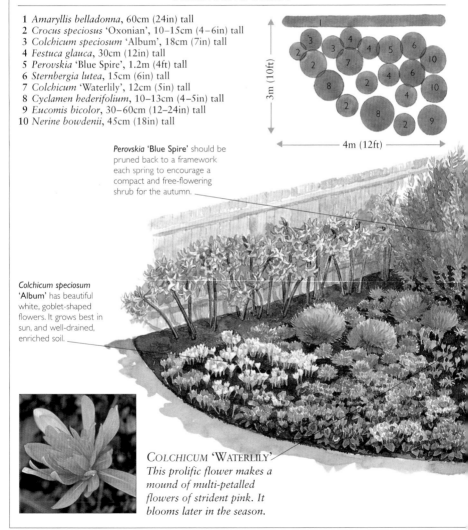

3m (10ft)

4m (12ft)

Perovskia '**Blue Spire**' should be pruned back to a framework each spring to encourage a compact and free-flowering shrub for the autumn.

Colchicum speciosum '**Album**' has beautiful white, goblet-shaped flowers. It grows best in sun, and well-drained, enriched soil.

COLCHICUM 'WATERLILY'
This prolific flower makes a mound of multi-petalled flowers of strident pink. It blooms later in the season.

MORE CHOICES

TALL
(over 90cm/36in)
Eucomis pole-evansii
Lilium formosanum
Lilium speciosum var. *rubrum*

MEDIUM
(30–90cm/12–36in)
Colchicum 'Pink Goblet'

Colchicum speciosum
Nerine bowdenii 'Alba'

SMALL
(below 30cm/12in)
Crocus kotschyanus
Crocus ochroleucus
Cyclamen cilicium

AMARYLLIS BELLADONNA
Tall stems are topped with
funnels of pink, which
seem to be triggered into
flowering by heavy rain in
late summer.

Nerine bowdenii
flowers best in dry
sunny spots that
are shunned by
other plants.

STERNBERGIA LUTEA
A strong yellow goblet,
which is quite an unusual
colour for an autumn bulb.
It thrives in full sun.

Eucomis bicolor is a large South
African bulb that flowers in late
summer. It grows best in well-
fertilized soil in full sun. The
succulent leaves grow throughout the summer and need
watering in a drought. It has
quite attractive seed capsules,
which can be removed if seed
is not required.

Crocus speciosus 'Oxonian' is a dark
violet crocus planted to best effect
close together in groups or drifts.

Festuca glauca is an attractive,
evergreen grass which is easily
grown and never becomes a
nuisance by seeding or running.

Cyclamen hederifolium
comes from around the
Mediterranean, but is totally
hardy and at home in
temperate gardens.

A WINTER BORDER

There is a surprisingly wide range of winter-flowering bulbs to be considered. An island bed such as this is best positioned close to a paved walkway for easy access in damp weather. The structure provided by deciduous shrubs and small trees is ideal because it casts shade for the bulbs when they are resting. The shrubs also provide an attractive and natural background for the delicate-looking woodland and meadow bulbs.

MORE CHOICES

MEDIUM
(30–90cm/12–36in)
Narcissus 'Rijnveld's
  Early Sensation'

SMALL
(below 30cm/12in)
Corydalis malkensis

Crocus sieberi 'Albus'
  C. sieberi 'Violet
  Queen'
Galanthus elwesii
  G. 'Magnet'
  G. nivalis
  G. plicatus

Acer davidii, snake-bark maple, is a small deciduous tree ideally suited to smaller gardens. It has the bonus of attractive bark.

LEUCOJUM VERNUM
The snowflakes are taller and larger than snowdrops but equally attractive and easy to establish.

Philadelphus coronarius is a shrub which has scented white flowers in summer. It can be pruned annually to keep an attractive framework.

Eranthis hyemalis, or winter aconite, quickly opens as the days lengthen. Each flower is framed by a ruff of leaves.

PLANTING PLAN

1 *Galanthus plicatus* subsp. *byzantinus*, 20cm (8in) tall
2 *Leucojum vernum*, 20–30cm (8–12in) tall
3 *Acer davidii*, 15m (50ft) tall
4 *Hamamelis mollis*, 4m (12ft) tall
5 *Philadelphus coronarius*, 3m (10ft) tall
6 *Eranthis hyemalis*, 5–8cm (2–3in) tall
7 *Scilla bifolia*, 8–15cm (3–6in) tall
8 *Cyclamen coum*, 5–8cm (2–3in) tall

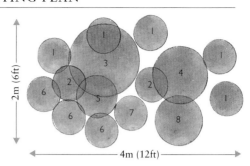

2m (6ft)

4m (12ft)

Hamamelis mollis, or witch hazel, has extraordinarily fragrant flowers, borne in late winter on leafless branches. They add much to any winter bed.

CYCLAMEN COUM
Short and hardy, these maroon, pink, or white flowers shine out during the dull winter days. The leaves vary from plain green to the near silver leaves of the Pewter Group.

Galanthus plicatus subsp. *byzantinus* is an early-flowering form of this variable and bold snowdrop. It has much larger leaves than the common snowdrop *G. nivalis*.

Scilla bifolia will seed around to form a beautiful blue carpet of starry bells.

A LAYERED BORDER

This is a border where the use of bulbs means that colour and shape can be achieved from winter through to late spring. The border rises in height as the seasons progress, with the earlier flowering bulbs hidden by the taller spring flowers. Once late spring arrives, the border will need to be cleared of foliage and tidied, to allow late perennials and a few colourful annuals to provide the necessary summer and autumn interest.

MORE CHOICES

TALL (over 90cm/36in)
Allium hollandicum
Cardiocrinum giganteum
Lilium martagon

MEDIUM
(30–90cm/12–36in)
Anemone pavonina
Leucojum vernum
Tulipa praestans 'Fusilier'

SMALL (below
30cm/12in)
Galanthus elwesii
Muscari armeniacum
Narcissus 'Tête-à-tête'

ERYTHRONIUM REVOLUTUM
A choice bulb that sets a modest amount of seed and so can slowly build into a colony.

Muscari azureum is another small spreader that seeds profusely. It has a true blue flower in early spring.

Fritillaria imperialis has large heads of hanging bells, available in yellow to dark orange.

Galanthus nivalis is a snowdrop, impervious to cold weather and excellent in drifts.

Anemone blanda is a reliable, low-growing, daisy-like flower that may start flowering in late winter, if the weather is mild.

Corydalis malkensis is an amazing carpeter that flowers right through the spring.

Ipheion uniflorum 'Wisley Blue' has light blue trumpets held above attractive leaves for a long period in spring.

Scilla bifolia appears very early and has eye-catching bright blue petals and attractive anthers.

PLANTING PLAN

1 *Anemone blanda*, 15cm (6in) tall
2 *Galanthus nivalis*, 10cm (4in) tall
3 *Fritillaria imperialis*, 1.5m (5ft) tall
4 *Erythronium revolutum*, 20–30cm (8–12in) tall
5 *Corydalis solida*, 25cm (10in) tall
6 *Muscari azureum*, 10cm (4in) tall
7 *Fritillaria persica* 'Adiyaman', 1.5m (5ft) tall
8 *Tulipa linifolia* Batalinii Group, 35cm (14in) tall
9 *Ornithogalum nutans*, 20–60cm (8–24in) tall
10 *Corydalis malkensis*, 8–15cm (3–6in) tall
11 *Ipheion uniflorum* 'Wisley Blue', 15–20cm (6–8in) tall
12 *Scilla bifolia*, 8–15cm (3–6in) tall
13 *Anemone coronaria*, 30–45cm (12–18in) tall
14 *Iris* 'Katharine Hodgkin', 12cm (5in) tall
15 *Puschkinia scilloides*, 20cm (8in) tall

1.8m (6ft)
3m (10ft)

Tulipa linifolia Batalinii Group are reliable tulips that range from red through to cream, or a mix of both.

Fritillaria persica 'Adiyaman' is quite a tall plant with very attractive plum coloured bells on each stem. It may need supporting.

Corydalis solida is most attractive in its red-, pink-, or white-flowered forms.

IRIS 'KATHARINE HODGKIN'
This iris is popular for its unique colours and weather-proof properties early in the year.

Anemone coronaria flowers very early in the year if in full sun. It is best grown in very fast-draining soil.

Ornithogalum nutans is almost silvery in sunlight. This is a low-key but attractive member of the mostly white genus.

Puschkinia scilloides are very easy to grow. The flowers have white stripes on a blue background, and are good in sun or part shade.

BULBS IN FORMAL BEDS

These small formal plantings look stunning positioned close to buildings. Any edging plants need to be naturally small. Lavender and santolina can provide a silver frame, while a small, purple berberis gives a more sombre edge. The hyacinth bed will need foliar feeding once the flowers fade in order to ensure good flowering the following year. Large containers, such as barrels, can be used to produce a similar effect in miniature.

PLANTING PLAN

1 *Tulipa* 'Purissima', 35cm (14in) tall
2 *Fritillaria imperialis* 'Maxima Lutea', 1.5m (5ft) tall
3 *Tulipa* 'Queen of Sheba', 60cm (24in) tall
4 *Myosotis sylvatica* 'Blue Ball', 25cm (10in) tall

2m (6ft)

2m (6ft)

TULIPA 'QUEEN OF SHEBA'
Quite a tall tulip, with gracefully reflexed petals of scarlet bronze, with edges of golden yellow.

Fritillaria imperialis 'Maxima Lutea' is very impressive planted close together, with the pineapple tufts of leaves above the hanging bell flowers.

Myosotis sylvatica 'Blue Ball', or Forget-me-not, is an excellent bedding plant. It is hardy and in flower for a long period from late spring into summer.

PLANTING PLAN

1 *Hyacinthus orientalis* 'Anna Marie', 20–30cm (8–12in) tall
2 *H. orientalis* 'Delft Blue', 20–30cm (8–12in) tall
3 *H. orientalis* 'White Pearl', 20–30cm (8–12in) tall

MORE CHOICES

SMALL (below 30cm/12in)
Hyacinthus orientalis 'Carnegie'
H. orientalis 'City of Haarlem'
H. orientalis 'L'Innocence'
H. orientalis 'Ostara'

1.5m (5ft)

1.5m (5ft)

Hyacinthus orientalis 'Delft Blue' is nearly the colour of the famous china. It is a very reliable selection that is ideal for bedding.

Hyacinthus orientalis 'Anna Marie' is a light pink selection of this hardy bulb. Flowering times can be varied throughout spring, depending on the time of planting.

Hyacinthus orientalis 'White Pearl' is used in this formal structure, for the stark white needed to complete the trio.

Tulipa 'Purissima' is a Fosteriana hybrid with beautiful, sturdy milk-white flowers. It provides an ideal contrast to the more stridently coloured varieties.

MORE CHOICES

TALL (over 90cm/36in)
Fritillaria imperialis 'Rubra'
F. imperialis 'The Premier'

MEDIUM
(30–90cm/12–36in)
Tulipa 'Golden Apeldoorn'
T. 'Queen of Night'
T. 'White Triumphator'

SMALL (below 30cm/12in)
Muscari armeniacum
Narcissus 'Tête-à-tête'

Bulbs in Containers

For small gardens, or for an area of a larger garden that is frequently used, such as a patio, a display of bulbs in pots makes an eye-catching feature. The display should be in a sheltered spot and it is wise to take some precautions against wind damage. The pots can be discreetly hooked to each other for stability, or heavy pebbles can be used as top dressing or wedged around the bases. When buying pots, look for those that have a wide base.

PLANTING PLAN

1 *Dahlias* Unwins Dwarf Group, 60cm (24in) tall
2 *Lobularia maritima*, 5–30cm (2–12in) tall
3 *Canna*, 70cm (28in) tall
4 *Galtonia candicans*, 1–1.2m (3–4ft) tall
5 *Crocosmia* × *crocosmiiflora* 'Gerbe d'Or', 50cm–1.5m (20in–5ft) tall
6 *Lysimachia nummularia* 'Aurea', 5cm (2in) tall
7 *Allium moly*, 15–25cm (6–10in) tall
8 *Crocosmia* × *crocosmiiflora* 'Jackanapes', 40cm–60cm (16–24in) tall
9 *Lobelia erinus* 'Cambridge Blue', 10–23cm (4–9in) tall

Allium moly is a yellow-flowered onion and is very vibrant. It seeds modestly.

Crocosmia × *crocosmiiflora* 'Gerbe d'Or' is a very reliable plant that needs plenty of moisture and sunlight to display at its best.

Dahlias Unwins Dwarf Group make ideal container plants because they will flower for a long time if deadheaded and fed.

Lobularia maritima are dwarf white or pale purple-pink annuals that can be sown in spring to flower that summer. Trim after flowering to encourage further flowers.

Lysimachia nummularia 'Aurea' is a very easy and reliable herbaceous perennial which has bright yellow flowers over a long period in summer.

MORE CHOICES

TALL (over 90cm/36in)
Allium hollandicum 'Purple
  Sensation'
Lilium Golden Splendor
  Group
L. speciosum var. *rubrum*

MEDIUM
(30–90cm/12–36in)
Camassia leichtlinii
  'Semiplena'
Nerine bowdenii
Tulipa linifolia

SMALL
(below 30cm/12in)
Anemone coronaria
  cultivars
Colchicum 'Waterlily'
C. speciosum 'Album'

CROCOSMIA ×
CROCOSMIIFLORA
'JACKANAPES'
*This is one of the larger-
flowered hybrids. It can be
a little tender in an open
border and is best suited
to being grown in a pot
in cooler areas.*

Galtonia candicans
look almost succulent
in growth and have
beautiful pendent
bells on a tall spire.

Cannas are stately plants,
good for the back of the
display. They will flower
for months if kept fed
and watered.

Mixed lobelias
These perennials are
usually used for annual
bedding or container
planting.

LOOKING AFTER YOUR BULBS

WHEN TO BUY BULBS

THE BEST TIME TO SHOP FOR BULBS is as soon as they are available in garden centres, usually from late summer onwards. In early summer, to coincide with the annual flower shows, bulb catalogues appear and orders are sent out in two postings: the first in late summer and early autumn, for autumn-flowering plants, and the second from early to late autumn, for spring- and summer-flowering bulbs.

BUYING TIPS

The established mail-order bulb nurseries have a reputation to maintain, and usually their bulbs are of flowering size and in good condition. Other outlets may not always be as satisfactory, particularly with regard to the naming of stocks. In garden centres, the presentation of bulbs is colourful and informative, with the bulbs in aerated bags behind photographs of their flowers. Do look closely at the bulbs, because after a few weeks some may begin to deteriorate and even attempt to flower. Choosing bulbs from a basket (wearing gloves to avoid any possible irritation) is still the best and safest method of selection.

CHOOSING HEALTHY BULBS

• Always buy early and choose plump bulbs for immediate planting.

• Check the size. Small bulbs certainly will not flower in the first year.

• The outer tunic, or skin, should be intact and clean; it is the bulb's defence against desiccation.

• Diseased bulbs may smell unpleasant even before they show signs of deterioration.

• Reject bulbs that are in growth or have attempted to grow and then dried through lack of moisture.

Growing point should be firm

► TESTING A BULB
Gently squeeze a bulb to check that it is firm – an indication that it is healthy.

Basal plate should be firm and unblemished

▲ A GOOD BULB
The bulb should be of an even colour, with no stripes or blotches, and should look healthy, without any premature leaf or root growth.

◄ LEAFY BULBS
Snowdrop and snowflake bulbs must not dry out, so they are sold with their leaves for immediate planting.

◄ BLUEBELL WALK *A stone path, dappled in shade, winds through a sea of bluebells.*

PREPARING THE PLANTING SITE

T HE VAST MAJORITY OF BULBS come from soils that dry out to some degree during their resting period. In temperate climates, there are no regular dry periods, so to prevent the bulbs getting too wet, you must ensure the soil is free-draining. Before planting, heavy clay soil should be deeply dug to aerate the structure and coarse grit incorporated. On sandy soils, organic matter, like leafmould and well-rotted garden compost, will improve the nutrient levels.

ADDING NUTRIENTS BEFORE PLANTING

Bulbs are no different in their requirements for nutrients than other plants, but they do root in the same area just under the basal plate every year. To encourage continued flowering, nutrients can be added during a bulb's resting period. Organic material, such as garden compost, mushroom compost, and well-rotted manure, may be lightly forked into the bed. In a rock garden or raised bed, it may be more convenient to work in a concentrated fertilizer.

HANDLING FERTILIZER
• Always read the instructions carefully.
• Wear gloves. The latex type allow for good dexterity and are cheap enough to dispose of.
• Open and dispense in the open air to avoid breathing in any dust from the packaging.
• Dispose of empty containers or, if only part used, store in a dry, secure place.
• If mixed with water, use in a single application, because particles tend to settle.

CONCENTRATED FERTILIZERS

Organic concentrated fertilizers release nutrients slowly. These nutrients are accessible to plants as the ground warms in spring. They are best gently stirred into the soil, rather than simply scattered on top, and can be incorporated deeply at planting time. If you are concerned about the health risks of using these products, rock phosphate and seaweed meal are suitable alternatives. Inorganic fertilizers are released into the soil only once they are dissolved by either rainfall or hand watering. The pellets must not rest on any foliage, because the chemicals released soon kill any plant tissue they touch.

BLOOD, FISH, AND BONE

BONE MEAL

TYPES OF FERTILIZER
Always apply at the rate indicated on the container. It is useful to mix the fertilizer with coarse grit at planting time.

FORKING OVER THE GROUND
Concentrated fertilizers should be worked into the planting site with a fork to ensure they are incorporated into the soil.

PLANTING DEPTHS

Once the site has been well prepared, the pleasure of planting can begin. Most bulbs need to be planted at about two to three times their own depth in the ground. There are exceptions, however: tulips should be planted at about four times their own depth, while rhizomes of the wood anemone need to be placed just below the surface of the soil in well-rotted garden compost. If you find that a plant fails to flower, experiment by planting the bulb more deeply; this sometimes stops the bulb splitting into smaller offsets and may induce flowering.

In light, sandy soils it is best to plant more deeply but, whatever the soil, space the bulbs about two to three bulb-widths apart, then firm the site and water in. Some bulbs, like bluebells, have specially adapted, strong roots to help the bulbs find their own level.

BULB DEPTHS
Although a depth of 2–3 times their own height is sufficient for most bulbs, others need to be planted deeper, at 4 times their height. Bulbs flower more regularly if planted at greater depths where they are less affected by climatic changes.

Bulb planted at four times its depth

PREPARATION FOR NATURALIZING BULBS

The autumn is the best time for planting bulbs in naturalized situations. Wait for damp conditions when the disturbed grass will soon grow back and the ground will be easier to cultivate. If groups of small bulbs like crocuses or fritillaries are to be planted, use a spade to cut an H-shape in the grass, cut under the turf, and fold it back to reveal the soil. The soil can be loosened, fertilized, and the bulbs planted. The turf flaps are then folded back and the area well watered. If larger bulbs are to be planted, then a bulb-planting tool, which can take out a plug of soil 15cm (6in) deep, is best used. A little fertilizer should be added to the soil before the bulb is planted.

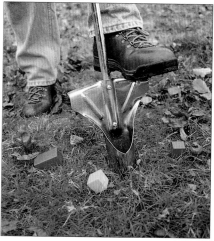

1 **To plan the display** but still retain a natural look, randomly scatter coloured blocks to represent the colours of the flowers.

2 **Then use a bulb** planter to make holes in the places indicated by the coloured blocks. A hand-sized version of this tool is available.

PLANTING BULBS

BULBS ARE QUICK TO GIVE A COLOURFUL DISPLAY wherever they are planted. This near-instant effect gives the new gardener encouragement and the experienced gardener a chance to move bulbs regularly, without any detrimental effect. Bulbs are among the few plants that are actually improved by being moved, split up, and replanted annually. Container bulbs can be planted straight out into the border as soon as the flowers have finished in late spring.

PLANTING "IN THE GREEN"

Bulbs that are prone to desiccation, such as snowdrops, snowflakes, and aconites, are best planted just after flowering, with the leaves intact, called "in the green". Plant these bulbs in soil that has been loosened and fertilized, making sure that they never dry out. To avoid any chance of infection, dust any wounded surfaces of the bulbs with a fungicide powder, such as yellow sulphur, before planting. Be careful to plant the bulbs back at their original depth. There is a papery sheath around the bulb that should be just visible when planting.

IN THE GREEN
The new planting depth should match the old. Aim for the point where the leaf meets the papery sheath at the top of the bulb. Spread out the roots, and always water the site well.

PLANTING IN THE OPEN

Try to find a site that is suitable for the bulbs you are planting. Most will need full exposure to the sun, but a few, such as camassias, prefer a shady site. Dig the site, remove any roots, and fork over the base of the site to aerate the land deeply. Add a dry fertilizer and place your bulbs in a hole of the correct depth. To achieve a random pattern, dig an irregular shaped hole. If large single bulbs are being planted, then a bulb planter makes the job easier, but a slim spade or trowel will suffice.

1 **Fork over the area,** then dig the hole to the depth required (2–3 times the bulb's depth). Add the dry fertilizer (*see inset*), and place the bulbs in the hole.

2 **Arrange the bulbs at random,** making sure that they remain upright as you replace the soil. Cover the bulbs and firm gently, then label the area.

PLANTING IN A CONTAINER

Most bulbs are suitable for growing in a container as long as the pot is large enough for the chosen bulb, and the drainage is adequate, or the roots may rot. As soon as the flowers are over, the pots can be placed out of sight. Always give the bulbs as much depth for root growth as possible as this reduces the watering needs. Try to use a soil-based compost, which will retain moisture and plant food for longer than a soilless one. Plant the bulbs as deeply as in the garden and cover the surface with a 4–5mm (⅛–¼in) layer of grit. This prevents soil splashing and reduces evaporation.

Bulbs should point upwards. This is not easy to tell with tubers such as corydalis.

1 **Lay some crocks** in the base before adding the compost. Place the bulbs on top of the compost with their growing points upwards.

2 **Top dress with grit**, and water well to settle the compost. Insert a label to identify the bulbs. Keep the soil moist.

BURYING A CONTAINER IN A BORDER

This is an excellent method of discreetly filling gaps or of bringing about seasonal changes within a border. The container can be a simple plastic pot or a lattice basket more usually used for pond plantings. The lattice baskets must be buried at all times, because the roots will be active beyond the confines of the basket, and so a resting place in the garden is needed for when the containers are not in season. The area around the sunken pots needs aerating with grit and compost so that any lifting and replanting does as little damage to the roots as possible. These baskets are also very useful for keeping track of your bulbs.

Check the bulbs are upright

1 **Plant the bulbs** at the usual depth in a compost to suit them and a bulb's width apart to allow for growth. The basket can be left in for a year or so to mature.

2 **Bury the basket** just below the surface of the ground, fix a label to the basket, and water in. A bark mulch is an attractive and easily removed top-dressing.

ROUTINE CARE

ONCE BULBS ARE PLANTED, they provide years of pleasure, requiring little aftercare. In summer, when the foliage has died down, it is best to remove the leaves and rake over the resulting holes in the ground to stop insects having access to the bulbs. After a few years, even if the bulbs are doing well, any dense clumps may need thinning out. Lift during the resting season, separate out, and replant. Tender bulbs, such as gladioli, need lifting before the onset of winter.

SUPPORTING

It would be marvellous if all bulbous plants could be freestanding, without artificial aid but, unfortunately, this is not the case and a few do need extra support. Vulnerable plants that may need staking are lilies, gladioli, dahlias, and some camassias. In pots, hyacinths and narcissi will need a little light tying. There are many commercial supports available – hoops, half-circles, Y-stakes, and grids of various types – and these are mostly discreet and reusable. However, many gardeners still rely on the traditional cane-and-twine method to hold the stem or stems. Soft, green jute is still the most unobtrusive twine for this work. Whatever you plan, start early, getting the structure in place before the wind damages the plant. In an emergency the half-circle and Y-stakes can be eased into position to support the stems that have begun to lean.

▲ STAKING A GLADIOLUS
Insert the cane next to the stem when 15cm (6in) tall and tie with soft garden twine in a figure-of-eight loop. When the plant is at bud stage, tie again just below the bud.

◄ STAKING A GROUP OF LILIES
Some lilies can be supported by carefully pushing in canes among the bulbs and tying in each stem with a figure-of-eight loop. When mature, the lilies will help support each other.

Feeding after Flowering

When the flowers begin to fade, the leaves will continue to work at building up the strength of the bulb.

To aid this process, a regular dilute liquid feed that is high in potash (such as tomato fertilizer) is very beneficial. This feeding will have the effect of prolonging the above-ground life of the plant, and will build up larger bulbs with the potential to flower and form offsets. Watering with a liquid fertilizer can also rectify any trace element deficiency in the soil, such as a lack of magnesium, which can lead to premature yellowing of the leaves. Once the leaves begin to decay, cease watering, because the bulbs will need a dry period in the summer.

LIQUID FEEDING
Make the feed half the recommended strength for tomatoes, and water the plants in early morning or evening so the leaves do not scorch.

Mulching

During the resting period, mulch bulb areas with well-rotted organic material, such as mushroom or garden compost. In the rock garden or raised bed, a finer mulch (graded by sieving) should be mixed with balanced fertilizer then top-dressed with gravel.

APPLYING MULCH
Organic material is best applied when bulbs are resting but can be added at other times as long as the soil is moist.

Using Inorganic Fertilizer

Commercially available preparations, such as tomato feed or pelleted fertilizer, enable the gardener to add precisely, by dilution with water, the desired amount of fertilizer to the plant at the required intervals. Always read the instructions carefully and use the fertilizer regularly at greater dilution rather than in one large dose. If the soil is dry, dampen it first, otherwise the fertilizer may run off the area away from the plant. Never water chemicals directly onto foliage in direct sunlight, because this will scorch the leaves. In free-draining sandy soils, much of the nutrient content of the fertilizer may be washed away very quickly by heavy rain.

TYPES OF INORGANIC FERTILIZERS

• Tomato fertilizer is high in potash and ideal for promoting flower production in bulbs.

• Granular fertilizers have an even spread of nitrogen, phosphate, and potash for general feeding.

• Specialist fertilizers come in combinations of nitrogen, phosphate, and potash in ratios to suit all plants. The ratio of 15:15:30 is ideal for bulbs. These mixes contain trace elements essential for healthy growth.

TOMATO FERTILIZER

WHEN TO TIDY LEAVES

RESIST THE TEMPTATION to remove the foliage soon after the flowers have faded, because this will weaken the bulb and reduce the flowering next season. Wait until the foliage is just turning yellow before you remove it, because green leaves are helping to build up the bulb for next year. The leaves die down at differing rates, with corydalis and snowdrops ready for clearing by late spring, whereas colchicum leaves must wait until early summer.

REMOVING FOLIAGE

While the leaves are yellow, some will still cling to the bulb, so if you pull them off, you risk bringing the dormant bulb to the surface. It is, therefore, better to cut off the foliage. Some summer-flowering bulbs, such as alliums and camassias, have leaves that are already dying down at flowering time. If they are not hidden by other foliage, you can cut them off without detriment to the bulb.

CUTTING BACK TO THE GROUND
Naturalized bulb foliage is best cut off to ground level using shears. This removes the surrounding grass and tidies the site.

LIFTING BULBS

After a few years, the flowering display of a group of bulbs may begin to wane, indicating that it is time to lift and thin the bulbs. While the bulbs are resting, insert a fork some distance back from the clump, and lift. The bulbs will probably be very congested and of many sizes.

Most gardeners will simply replant the largest and healthiest bulbs in a fresh part of the garden. If large numbers are wanted, the smaller bulbs and the offsets from the larger ones can be grown on in a nursery patch. After a few seasons they will start to flower and can be moved.

MOVING BULBS "IN THE GREEN"

You may need to move plants during the "wrong" season, while they are still green. Treat them like other plants: dig up the root ball intact and replant immediately. Water well. You could pot up the bulb and keep it in a shady place until it dies down naturally.

MOVING "IN THE GREEN"
When bulbs, such as daffodils, are dying down, they can be carefully lifted and placed in a box to dry out prior to cleaning and storage.

STORING BULBS

BULBS USED IN CONTAINERS or in any form of seasonal bedding may need to be stored safely until they are replanted in the next season. If you need to clear part of the garden by moving bulbs while the leaves are still green, be careful to lift the root ball intact and replant in a pot or shady part of the garden. Label the spot and keep it watered until the leaves begin to decay. Once the leaves have turned yellow, the bulbs can then be lifted and prepared for storage.

STORAGE CONDITIONS

Most bulbs, like tulips, crocuses, and daffodils, can be stored. Dry bulbs are best stored in a paper bag or cardboard box, labelled, and kept in a cool, airy place. Check them every few weeks and remove any bulbs that show signs of rotting.

There are a few bulbs, however, such as erythroniums and wood anemones, that need cool, moist conditions to remain in good health. These bulbs can be lifted in the same way, but need setting in a pot of rich compost or a reserve bed, and should be labelled ready for careful lifting when required. Alternatively, these bulbs can be mixed with a little vermiculite, placed in a clean plastic bag, and stored at 6°C (43°F). (A salad container in a refrigerator is also ideal for this purpose.)

1 **Clean off any soil** by hand or with a dry paintbrush and remove the old foliage and any old dried roots. Keep only the healthy, unblemished bulbs.

2 **Make sure** that the bulbs are clean and dry before dusting them with a fungicide. Shake off any excess, place in a clean paper bag, and label. Keep them cool and dry.

WINTER STORAGE
Most bulbs, such as daffodils, can be stored in dry, cool conditions until needed. Use a cardboard or wooden box kept in dark, dry place.

STORING BULBS

• Select only the best bulbs.
• Corms such as gladioli should be placed in a box to dry out prior to cleaning and storage.
• Dip dry corms and tubers in fungicide to avoid rotting.
• To store gladiolus corms, snap the old corms from the new, discarding the old ones and keeping the new corms dry and frost-free until replanted.
• Check regularly for disease.

FORCING PREPARED BULBS

A LONG-ESTABLISHED PRACTICE is to plant specially prepared bulbs in containers and keep them in the dark to induce them to flower early, providing colour and cheer during the winter months. Hyacinths and some daffodils are favourites for this treatment. Initially grown in the dark, they are best moved to a cool room or conservatory once the leaves begin to show, and brought into the living room only for the period of flowering, when the flowers and scent can be enjoyed.

HYACINTHS

Prepared hyacinths should be bought as soon as they appear in the garden centre or nursery and planted in bulb fibre compost, close together, with the tips of the bulbs just showing above the compost. Water so that the compost is damp, but not soggy. Place in a cool dark cupboard or inside a black plastic bag kept in a garage or cellar, and continue to keep the compost just moist. After about eight weeks, the bud will be visible and it is time to bring the plant into a light, but not sunny, position to flower. A cool room or conservatory is ideal. If they begin to lean, tie to a central cane.

SEASONAL FAVOURITES

As long as the selection is marked as a "prepared" bulb you can be sure of very early, midwinter flowering.

Prepared hyacinths include **'Anna Marie'**, a soft pink, **'L'Innocence'**, which is compact and white, and **'Ostara'**, a deep blue.
There are also multiflora hyacinths with a similar colour range available.

Prepared daffodils like **'Paper White'** and **'Grand Soleil d'Or'** should be started in bright but not strong light. They are best grown in cool rooms so they do not become lanky and so need staking.

A 15cm (6in) pot will accommodate 3 hyacinth bulbs

At this stage of growth, the pot can be brought into a light, cool room

1 Choose an attractive container and plant three or five bulbs in moist bulb fibre compost, with their tips just visible. Place in a cool dark place.

2 When the flower buds are visible, albeit rather yellow, bring them into a cool, but bright position to grow quickly and flower. They will soon turn green in the light.

GROWING BULBS IN WATER

This method is ideal for children, because plant growth can so easily be seen. A glass or plastic container should be filled to the neck with water to which a few pieces of charcoal are added, in order to keep the water clear and sweet smelling. Always use prepared hyacinth bulbs and set them in a cool, dark place, as for soil-planted bulbs. Once the bulb has strong root growth, it can then be placed on a bright, but not sunny, windowsill to flower. The only care needed is to top up of the water level. Once the bulb has flowered, it is best discarded.

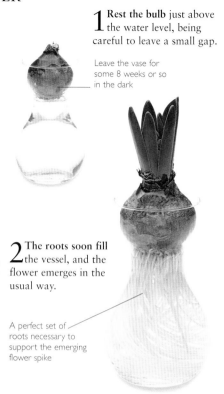

1 Rest the bulb just above the water level, being careful to leave a small gap.

Leave the vase for some 8 weeks or so in the dark

CARE IN WATER

• Keep the water topped up to just beneath the basal plate.
• If the water starts to smell, replace it with fresh water as you would for cut flowers.
• Regularly turn the container to keep the flower stem upright and stable.
• Although the bulb could be grown on, it has been without nutrients and is best discarded once the flower is finished. If you want to plant it out, do so carefully, spreading the roots, and water in.

2 The roots soon fill the vessel, and the flower emerges in the usual way.

A perfect set of roots necessary to support the emerging flower spike

FORCING HIPPEASTRUM

The large-flowered hippeastrums are very versatile plants, and it is now possible to buy and flower them at any time of the year. There are colours ranging from pure white through pink to a strong red, and smaller multi-flowered varieties, all of which are equally easy to grow and flower. Garden centres stock hippeastrums in autumn as colourfully boxed kits. Unlike the other forced bulbs, these need warm and light conditions from the beginning to flower and grow well. When grown near a window, they do require turning to straighten the flowering stem. Keep the plant cool (10°C/50°F) through the autumn until midwinter, when the leaves can be trimmed to 10cm (4in) and the top of the old compost replaced with new. Bring into the warm and start regular watering and feeding. These bulbs should only be repotted in their third year.

COMMERCIALLY AVAILABLE KITS
Plant the large bulbs with only the bottom half covered by the compost. Water sparingly until the leaves and roots are well developed.

Kits include compost, cultural instructions, and a pot as well as the bulb

GROWING YOUR OWN BULBS

M OST BULBS NATURALLY MULTIPLY to survive. To obtain more plants, the gardener simply has to tap into this process at the appropriate time. Bulbs can be teased apart and the colony enlarged, but tubers, such as aconites, need to be cut into smaller pieces if more plants are required. During dormancy is usually the best time to propagate bulbs, and this is most easily achieved by lifting the whole clump, gently it teasing apart, and replanting the most healthy bulbs.

STARTING BULBS FROM SEED

This is another simple but effective method of propagation. Collect the seed in paper bags, so that any excess moisture is absorbed by the paper and does not lead to the seeds rotting. Bulb seed is usually quite large and easily handled, but it does need cleaning before being sown. Tip the seed onto a tray and gently winnow to remove the chaff and infertile seed. Then sow in a prepared pot or store the seed in a dry, airy, shaded spot, such as a shed, until sowing time. This is generally in early autumn for germination the following spring.

▶ GATHERING A RIPE SEEDHEAD
Take the bag to the seedhead, so seeds are not lost as the head is snapped from the stem. Shake the head to release the seeds.

1 Choose a pot to suit the number of seeds being sown. A 7cm (3in) pot will be adequate for up to 12 seeds, but do not sow them too closely or the potential growth will be inhibited.

2 Cover the seeds with 5mm (¼in) of sieved seed compost. Do not press down, but just tap the pot to settle the compost. Very large bulb seeds may need a greater depth of covering.

3 Cover the compost evenly with 5mm (¼in) of grit, so that the compost is hidden. This will deter the growth of liverwort and mosses and also protect the seeds from being dislodged during watering.

DIVIDING FLESHY-ROOTED BULBS

Some larger bulbs, such as lilies and nerines, have very thick fleshy roots that, although produced annually, persist as useless husks from year to year. Eventually, the soil needs refreshing around the bulbs and the old roots teasing out. When the bulbs are dying down, take a fork and carefully insert it some distance from the clump, then gently lift. You may find some active white roots among the old; try to keep these intact while you discard the old roots, leaves, and any damaged or diseased bulbs. From the remaining bulbs, plant only the best, in enriched soil, and water well. Cut dahlia tubers in half in spring, making sure each half has a growing point, and plant out.

1 **Divide a large area** into manageable clumps. Push the fork under the bulbs from one side, then repeat from another side if there is resistance. Lever the clump free of the soil.

2 **Separate out the bulbs,** once lifted, carefully prizing them apart by hand, if possible. Discard the old roots and leaves, but keep any young roots.

EASILY PROPAGATED BULBS

Some bulbs can be divided when resting. Offsets are attached to the sides of the parent bulb and can be eased apart and planted in their own space.
Galanthus (snowdrop)
Narcissus (daffodil)
Scilla

Some bulbs seed profusely: lift young bulbs as they are required. If you require more, collect ripe seedheads and sow them in a pot. Put the pot in a shady place.
Allium
Cyclamen
Eranthis

3 **Clean the bulbs gently.** Then select the very best bulbs for replanting in a newly prepared site. If the old site is to be reused, work in some bone meal or similar fertilizer as well as some new soil before planting.

Avoiding Problems

BULBS ARE NO MORE PRONE TO PROBLEMS than other plants. Always buy healthy, fresh stock for planting, and if you are given a suspect-looking bulb, harden your heart and get rid of it. Always dispose of any diseased bulbs by burning or placing in a sealed bag in the dustbin, never on the compost heap. Once you have healthy bulbs, good gardening habits will prevent many of the possible problems from occurring and reduce the need for any chemical or biological controls.

Identifying Problems

Any problem with a bulb results in poor or stunted growth. As soon as you see abnormal growth, lift the bulb with the surrounding soil and examine it carefully. It may be that the damage is physical, e.g., from a slug, or cultural. If the roots are short or non-existent, the drainage may need improving. Dig deeply and replant, watering the bulbs well. Occasionally, a stem may grow grotesquely as if many stems are fused together. This is fasciation and is not contagious. It is often the result of some damage in early growth.

Bulb Blindness

Occasionally, bulbs form buds that fail to flower. This is often a result of overcrowding and a lack of nutrients, it is rarely a disease. Bulb blindness is easily remedied by lifting and replanting in fertilized soil.

BASAL ROT
This fungal disease has no cure. Safe disposal (not on the compost heap) to stop it spreading to healthy bulbs is the only recourse.

A brown stain spreads around the scales of the bulb

Dealing with Pests

• Be vigilant and remove any pests by hand.
• Keep a tidy garden so that there are fewer places for pests to live and breed.
• Use pesticide sparingly as a last resort, avoiding contact with any other wildlife.
• In greenhouses, try simple traps, such as sticky papers, and other non-biological means of keeping pests in check.
• The introduction of predatory and parasitic insects to greenhouses can be an effective method of controlling specific pests (e.g. whitefly by a parasitic wasp).
• Encourage birds by setting up nestboxes. The blue tit will feed hundreds of caterpillars a day to its fledglings.

Bulb Flies

A number of insects use bulbs as a host in their lifecycle. The narcissus bulb fly looks like a small bumble bee and lays its eggs on the neck of the bulb in early summer. Mound soil over the holes left by the old stem and leaves as they die down. There may be remaining eggs or insects in the soil, so do not replant bulbs in the same area for several years or they may also be affected.

Storage Rot

Infections can enter bulbs and tubers like dahlias while they are in storage. Discard any rotting material before the disease has time to spread to other tubers and bulbs. If dry bulbs develop grey velvet mould (*botrytis*), they must be destroyed and adjacent bulbs dusted with fungicide.

A CALENDAR OF SEASONAL REMINDERS

SUMMER

• As the leaves of early-flowering bulbs die down, lift and divide any that are overcrowded.

• Collect dry seed in paper bags and store in a cool dry place. Remember to label the bags.

• Clear away dying foliage to tidy the border and avoid the spread of disease.

• Rake over holes left in the soil by old bulb stems to lessen the chance of insects like the pests narcissus bulb fly and ghost swift moth laying eggs in the tunnel, giving the larvae easy access to the bulb. Finally, mulch the whole area.

• Plant out pot-grown summer- and autumn-flowering bulbs to fill gaps in the border or to enhance a colour scheme.

• Repot winter and spring bulbs, now they are resting. Some may require completely repotting with new compost; others just need an inspection and topping up with fresh compost with some extra general-purpose fertilizer.

• Tie gladioli and tall dahlias to stakes for support.

• Buy new bulbs from your local garden centre or order from bulb catalogues.

AUTUMN

• Plant commercial bulbs as quickly as possible. Daffodils can begin root growth as early as late summer, if the conditions are right.

• Prepare heavy or compacted soil for planting by digging deeply, adding grit to aid aeration. Sprinkle a general-purpose fertilizer into the planting hole, and plant the bulbs at two or three times their own depth (or deeper, depending on the bulb; see p.51).

• Lift dahlias and gladioli and prepare for winter storage.

ADDING FERTILIZER

• Mark the location of your bulbs with labels or by drawing a plan, to avoid disturbance later.

• Make sure that there is sufficient space in the borders for autumn bulbs by tidying any summer foliage back so that the flowers can be enjoyed to the full.

• In early autumn, plant containers with specially-prepared bulbs to flower in midwinter.

WINTER

• Clear away any old foliage that might impede fresh growth, and mulch the site.

• Add a general-purpose fertilizer to the surrounding soil.

STORING BULBS OVER WINTER

• Store bulbs in a box in a cool, frost free place and check regularly for disease.

• It is possible to move groups of bulbs at this time of year. Dig up the clump and place in the new position. Water in to settle the roots and reduce the chance of stress through drought.

• Sow commercial bulb seed as soon as received and cover the compost with 5mm (¼in) grit to restrict evaporation and deter the growth of liverwort and moss. Expose the pots to the weather in a shady position.

• If leaves show signs of disease like streaking, lift the whole plant and dispose of it.

• Bring forced bulbs into a cool place to flower.

• Order late summer flowering bulbs.

SPRING

• Replant pot-grown bulbs bought for an instant effect, and water in.

• Snowdrops and snowflakes bought "in the green" should be planted without delay and copiously watered in.

• Check for any signs of grey mould (botrytis), especially prevalent if the season is dry, and consider spraying with a fungicide to reduce infection.

• In windy sites, stake tall bulbs, like crown imperials and lilies, before they are damaged.

• In late spring, plant out tender bulbs like gladioli and begonias.

• Deadhead flowers to concentrate energy into bulb development rather than seed production.

• In late spring, clear away the yellowing bulb foliage to tidy the border and to eliminate the homes for slugs and snails.

• Container bulbs grown for winter display can be stored in a cool out of the way place, until the time for repotting in summer.

• Feed potted bulbs with liquid fertilizer.

• Water indoor cyclamen as they get new leaves. Feed every two weeks.

CHOICE BULBS FOR THE GARDEN

THE FOLLOWING LIST is no more than a selection from the wide range of adaptable and easily grown bulbs for sale in nurseries and garden centres. Traditionally available in late summer and early autumn as dry bulbs, they are increasingly sold in pots as flowering plants, enabling the gardener to see their exact colour and height. The choice of bulbs is rich and diverse, and one that is not listed here is not necessarily inferior to another that is featured.

🞖 *Prefers full sun* 🞕 *Prefers partial shade* ◊ *Prefers well-drained soil* ◊ *Prefers moist soil* ❄❄❄ *Fully hardy (down to –20°C/–5°F)* ❄❄ *Frost-hardy (down to –5°C/23°F)* ❄ *Half-hardy (down to 0°C/32°F)* ❧ *Frost-tender* **Small** *Up to 30cm (12in)* **Medium** *30–90cm (12–36in)* **Tall** *Over 90cm (36in)* ♀ *RHS Award of Garden Merit*

A

Allium
Of the huge genus of onions, those of ornamental value have impressive flowerheads and strappy, pungent leaves. All of these species flower in summer and multiply quickly by seed, forming colonies. *A. cernuum* ♀ (nodding onion) is a small to medium grower with nodding flowers varying from white to rose-purple. 'Hidcote' ♀ is taller and plum-purple. 🞖◊ ❄❄–❧
A. cristophii ♀ is a medium onion with a 15cm (6in) flowerhead of metallic, pink-purple flowers. 🞖◊ ❄❄❄
A. hollandicum ♀, syn. *A. aflatunense* of gardens, is a tall onion, with a 10cm (4in) pink-purple head. 🞖◊ ❄❄❄

ALLIUM MOLY ♀

The flowerheads of both *A. cristophii* and the smaller *A. hollandicum* are excellent as dried-flower decorations. *A. moly* ♀ (golden garlic) is a small plant with bright yellow flowers in a 5cm (2in) flowerhead. 🞖◊ ❄❄❄

A. cristophii p.9
A. insubricum ♀ *p.37*
A. oreophilum ♀ *p.37*

Amaryllis
This is a genus of just one exotic-looking species that flowers in the early autumn. *A. belladonna* is a bulbous plant of medium height originating in South Africa, with thick, green-to-purple stems, and around six large, trumpet-shaped pink flowers, each up to 10cm (4in) long, that are produced in the autumn. The flowers are followed by long, strap-shaped leaves. Plant amaryllis on the sunny side of a wall to protect it against frost and to ripen the bulb. In cooler climates, amaryllis is best grown in a cool greenhouse. 🞖◊ ❄❄

◄ LILY-FLOWERED *KAUFMANNIANA* GROUP TULIPS *A beautiful yellow hybrid of medium height.*

ANEMONE CORONARIA
'LORD LIEUTENANT'

Anemone (Windflower)
This genus grows in varied habitats from cool woods to rocky mountains.
A. blanda ♀ is a small, tuberous plant with daisy-like flowers, up to 4cm (1½in) in diameter, in colours that vary from blue through purple to pink and white, often with a pale eye. It likes sun or partial shade, and spreads quickly by seed dispersal. ▣–▣◊ ❁❁❁
A. coronaria is a small to medium, tuberous plant with showy flowers, good for cutting, which can be red, blue, or white, in spring.
The De Caen Group and the St. Brigid Group are collective names for single-flowered and double-flowered selections of this species respectively, again with a wide colour range.
▣◊ ❁❁❁
A. nemorosa ♀ is a small, rhizomatous native wood anemone and has many garden cultivars in white and shades of blue, which brighten early spring. It has attractive, mid-green dissected foliage, once the flowers have finished. ▣◊ ❁❁❁

A. blanda p.8
A. pavonina p.9
Also recommended:
A. × *fulgens*

B

Begonia
Tuberous bedding begonias are essentially summer-flowering, mostly double-flowered hybrids, many with showy flowers, in a wide range of colours. They are small to medium in height. The tubers should be lifted in the autumn before the first frost, and stored frost-free until they are replanted in spring. ▣◊ ❁–♠
Multiflora Begonias *p.20*

C

Camassia (Quamash)
These bulbs flower in late spring to early summer. Their restrained shades and ease of cultivation mean that they are gaining popularity. They will thrive in any ordinary border and do not require a dry summer rest. *C. cusickii* is a

CAMASSIA LEICHTLINII

CANNA 'ASSAUT'

medium, meadowland bulb from North America. It has a few channelled leaves and tall spires of pale to deep blue, starry flowers. ▣◊ ❁❁
C. leichtlinii is taller, with creamy-white flowers. There is a double form 'Semiplena' in cultivation. ▣◊ ❁❁
C. quamash p.25

Canna (Indian shot plant)
These tall, rhizomatous plants have paddle-shaped leaves – themselves very architectural – topped with brightly coloured, three-petalled flowers in the summer. In frosty areas they should be lifted in autumn, stored in a frost-free environment (*see p.57*), and replanted in spring. 'Assaut' (*p.31*) has scarlet and orange flowers and purple-brown leaves.
'King Midas' has dark leaves and golden yellow flowers.
▣◊ ❁
Also recommended:
Tropicanna

Cardiocrinum (Giant lily)
This genus of three species is from South-east Asia. All are

tall plants that require rich soil, with moisture during the summer. These bulbs have perennial roots, which must not be allowed to dry out. They take several years to reach maturity and flower, after which they die, leaving several offsets.

C. giganteum ♥ has attractive, heart-shaped leaves, a tall stem up to 3m (10ft), and scented, trumpet-shaped flowers in summer. ◩◊ ❀❀

Chionodoxa
(Glory of the snow)
This genus from West Turkey, Crete, and Cyprus is related to *Scilla* (*p.76*). These small bulbous plants are easy to grow in sun or partial shade. They soon seed profusely, flowering quickly from seed.

C. luciliae ♥ has up to 12 small, starry, blue flowers per stem. A pink-flowered form is also available. ◩–◙◊ ❀❀❀

Colchicum (Naked ladies)
These corms are sometimes incorrectly referred to as the 'Autumn crocuses'. To add to the confusion, there are many autumn-flowering crocuses.

C. byzantinum ♥ is a small, prolific plant with soft lilac, starry flowers, 10cm (4in) in diameter, in the autumn. These are followed in spring by large, ribbed leaves. There is also a white form.

C. speciosum 'Album' ♥, also small, has white, goblet-shaped flowers on lime-green stems in autumn. They stand well for days, and are weather-resistant.

C. 'Waterlily' ♥ is small and vigorous, with up to five fully double, pinkish flowers per corm. Even when they fall over, the flowers remain attractive. These large-flowered selections look good on the sunny side of deciduous shrubs, or among herbaceous plants, which will disguise their dying leaves in summer. ◙◊ ❀❀❀

C. 'Waterlily' ♥ *p.38*
Also recommended:
C. tenorei ♥

Corydalis syn. *Pseudofumaria*
The tuberous corydalis is widespread in the northern hemisphere. The following are easy to grow, providing frost-hardy flowers in spring.

C. malkensis ♥, syn. *C. caucasica* var. *alba,* is small with creamy, tubular flowers in early spring. It is happy in sun or partial shade, and excellent for colonizing beds by seed. It blankets the ground in white, withering quickly in the late spring sun.

C. solida ♥, syn. *C. halleri,* also small, has flowers that vary from pink to red and purple, with some white examples. This small plant is best in full sun, where it remains compact and vibrant. ◩–◙◊ ❀❀❀

Crinum
Widespread in the southern hemisphere, crinums include one frost-hardy species.

C. × *powellii* ♥ is a tall South African hybrid and is just fully hardy if established in a well-drained, sheltered site. The long leaves are followed by tall stems topped with pink, fragrant, flared trumpets that are 10cm (4in) long. 'Album' ♥ is white. ◙◊ ❀❀❀

CARDIOCRINUM GIGANTEUM ♥

COLCHICUM SPECIOSUM 'ALBUM' ♥

CRINUM × POWELLII ♥

CROCUSES

All crocuses are small and can be chosen to provide colour in the open garden from autumn through to spring. ◊▣ ❀❀❀

Spring-flowering
Crocus ancyrensis has orange, rounded flowers. It is suited to a sunny bed or container.
C. chrysanthus '**Blue Pearl**' ♥ has white flowers that are overlaid with lilac-blue and have yellow throats.
C. chrysanthus '**Cream Beauty**' ♥ has a small, cream flower, with a deep yellow throat.
C. chrysanthus '**Ladykiller**' ♥ has flowers with a white background, and a purple mark on the outside.
C. × *luteus* '**Golden Yellow**' ♥ is a vigorous crocus, with orange-yellow flowers suitable for naturalizing.
C. sieberi '**Albus**', syn. 'Bowles White' ♥, is white with a yellow throat.

Crocus sieberi
'Hubert Edelsten' ♥

Crocus tommasinianus
'Ruby Giant' ♥

C. sieberi '**Hubert Edelsten**' ♥ is a pale lilac flower, with the three shining purple outer petals marked with a white line.
C. tommasinianus is a consummate survivor and spreader. There is an attractive white form **f.** *albus*.
C. tommasinianus '**Ruby Giant**' is sterile and good for light soil where seeding crocuses can be invasive.

Autumn-flowering
C. speciosus '**Oxonian**' is a dark violet crocus, up to 10cm (4in) tall. Its flowers are produced before the thin leaves appear in late winter. A good crocus for naturalizing in grass or around shrubs in light shade.
C. medius ♥ has bright purple flowers. It does well in sun or dappled shade.
C. ochroleucus ♥ produces its creamy-white flowers in late autumn.

Crocosmia × *crocosmiiflora*
'Star of the East'

Crocosmia (Montbretia)
This plant is easy to grow and forms self-supporting clumps. It is a medium-height plant, superb in sun or partial shade as long as the soil is well-drained, but moist. The corms grown are usually hybrids of the South African species.
C. × *crocosmiiflora* '**Dusky Maiden**' has unusual, deep bronze, lance-shaped leaves with funnel-shaped, brown-orange flowers in late summer.
C. × *crocosmiiflora* '**Star of the East**' is of medium height with starry, orange flowers, nearly 10cm (4in) across in late summer to early autumn.
C. '**Lucifer**' ♥ is tall and robust, with bright, deep-red flowers in midsummer.
▣–▣◊ ❀❀
C. × *crocosmiiflora*
   '**Gerbe d'Or**' *p.46*
   '**Jackanapes**' *p.47*
Also recommended:
C. × *crocosmiiflora*
'Emily McKenzie'

Cyclamen (Sowbread)
Beautiful tuberous plants that flower throughout the year. Many are scented.

C. coum ♀ is a small, late-winter flowering cyclamen. The round leaves can be anything from plain green to pewter colour, with every combination in-between, while the flowers range from white to carmine-red. These cyclamen are very effective when planted around deciduous shrubs, providing colour at the most drab time of year. ▨◊ ✳✳✳
C. hederifolium ♀ (syn. *C. neopolitanum*) is larger than *C. coum*, with triangular leaves and flowers produced in early autumn. They seed around very attractively once established, and look best planted in groups, rather than scattered. There is also an entirely silver-leaved selection, now widely available, which seems to produce mostly silver seedlings. ▨◊ ✳✳✳
C. persicum cultivars are sold as house plants in every florist and plant centre. The flowers range from white to carmine and vary greatly in shape. Once the flowers and leaves begin to wither, the plant should be rested away from sunlight and kept fairly dry. ▨◊❂ – ✳
C. cilicum p.39
C. coum p.11, p.41
C. hederifolium p.7
Also recommended:
C. repandum

Cyrtanthus (Fire lily)
A genus of tender bulbs from South Africa. The following species require a drier rest in winter, before growth and watering start in spring.
C. elatus (Scarborough lily) ♀ is a medium bulb that, in colder climates, makes an easy-to-grow and attractive

addition to the windowsill. This plant has strap-shaped leaves and scarlet, funnel-shaped flowers on stout stems in summer. ▨◊❂

D

Dahlia
Tuberous-rooted plants, from Central and South America, dahlias can be simply grouped into the tall border varieties and the shorter bedding types. There are thousands of cultivars of this plant with flowers in numerous colours, heights, and shapes. Dahlias flower from midsummer until the frosts of autumn, when the tubers should be lifted and stored frost-free *(see p.57)* and then replanted in the spring. Dahlias are hugely popular and the following is just a small selection of what is available.
'Bishop of Llandaff' ♀ is a medium to tall semi-double dahlia. It has red petals.
'Charlie Two' is a tall plant with medium-sized flowers. It has bright yellow, multi-petalled flowerheads.

Dahlia 'Fascination' ♀

'Fascination' ♀ is a small, peony-flowered bedding plant with dark pink flowers and dark bronze foliage.
'Glorie van Heemstede' ♀ is a bright yellow water-lily dahlia, of medium height.
'Grenidor Pastelle' is a bi-coloured dahlia of medium height and has a salmon-pink flower with a cream centre.
'Mi Wong' is a medium pompon dahlia with flowers that are strong pink in colour. ▨◊ ✳
Unwins Dwarf Group p.46
Also recommended:
'Arabian Night'

E

Eranthis (Winter aconite)
A tuberous plant, best in cool, semi-shaded positions.
E. hyemalis ♀ has yellow, cup-shaped flowers in spring. It is small, but in alkaline soils will spread quickly by seed in borders or in short grassland. Winter aconites are easy to incorporate in any garden, since, by mid-spring, foliage can be cleared away. ▨◊ ✳✳✳

Eranthis hyemalis ♀

EUCOMIS BICOLOR

Erythronium
(Dog's-tooth violet, Trout lily)

Bulbous plants with two basal leaves, mostly from North America, with a few from Europe and Asia. All erythroniums can be bought as pot plants or as slightly damp bulbs, as they resent being dried.
E. dens-canis ♀ is a small, spring-flowering plant with beautiful, mid-green leaves marbled purple-brown. The flowers, which are white, pink, or lilac, are pendent and arch gracefully backwards.
E. 'Pagoda' ♀ is a vigorous plant, with bronze-marked leaves and between two and five yellow flowers, each with a brown central ring. 'Pagoda' may grow to medium height.
E. revolutum (American trout lily) ♀ is a small but very beautiful plant, with bright green leaves and mottled brown and pink, backward arching flowers. This variety will seed to form a colony.
🖾◊ ✿✿✿
Also recommended:
E. californicum ♀

Eucomis (Pineapple flower, Pineapple lily)
These bulbs from South Africa have strong roots requiring lots of moisture. A medium, late-summer flowering bulb, *Eucomis bicolor* is nearly fully hardy, especially if given protective mulch in winter. The tall flower spikes have green flowers, each margined in purple, with a pineapple-like tuft of leaves at the top.
🖾◊ ✿✿
E. bicolor p.10
E. pole-evansii p.39

F

Fritillaria (Fritillary)
All plants in this genus have pendent, bell-shaped flowers. *F. imperialis* (Crown imperial) is a tall spring bulb, with whorls of leaves and stately flower spikes, each with up to eight hanging, bell-shaped flowers in yellow, orange, or red. Each flower stalk is topped with a tuft of leaves. *F. meleagris* ♀ (Snake's head fritillary) is a European

FRITILLARIA MELEAGRIS ♀

fritillary native to Britain, and tolerant of many garden situations – from a sunny border to naturalization in short grass. It is short-stemmed, with thin, greyish leaves, and has chequered, nodding, bell-shaped, purplish or white flowers in spring. *F. persica* 'Adiyaman' ♀ is a tall plant with a spire of up to 30 small purple bells in early spring above a tuft of grey-green leaves.
🖾◊ ✿✿✿
F. imperialis p.17
F. imperialis 'The Premier' *p.45*
F. imperialis 'Rubra' *p. 45*
F. pallidiflora p.18 ♀

G

Galanthus (Snowdrop)
This genus of small bulbs has white, bell-shaped flowers. Most are spring flowering, but a few flower in autumn. *G. elwesii* ♀ is a small plant, but it is a robust grower, with broad, glaucous leaves and a white, nodding flower. It likes a little more sun than some

GALANTHUS PLICATUS
SUBSP. *BYZANTINUS*

snowdrops. When happy, it regularly sets seed.

G. nivalis (Common snowdrop) ♀ is the beautiful harbinger of spring, and has become naturalized in many regions. It has a nodding, white flower with a small, green bridge on the inside. The leaves are quite narrow. These snowdrops are easy to cultivate and to naturalize. *G. plicatus* ♀ is a large snowdrop with turned-back margins to the leaves. This bulb quickly develops offsets. ▣◊ ❀❀❀

Also recommended: *G.* 'S. Arnott' ♀

Galtonia

A small South African genus of bulbs, summer-growing and well suited to a herbaceous border.

G. candicans is a medium plant that flowers in late summer. The head of up to 30 white, pendulous flowers is surrounded by long, grey-green leaves. Not dormant until well into autumn, it is sometimes sold in pots just prior to flowering. ▣◊ ❀❀❀

GALTONIA CANDICANS

IRISES

This is a large genus of bulbous and rhizomatous plants available in many shapes and colours. The Reticulate irises have simple netted bulbs, whereas the Juno irises have bulbs with long, fleshy roots. The Xiphium irises flower a little later in spring, and have larger bulbs.

Juno iris
I. bucharica ♀ is a vigorous iris of medium stature, with glossy, broad leaves beneath which are produced several large, creamy-white flowers with yellow blades to the falls (large, spreading outer petals). A sunny position with good, free-draining soil suits it well. ▣◊ ❀❀❀

Reticulate irises
'Harmony', a small iris, ideal for growing in containers or in the edge of a border. The flowers are royal-blue with a yellow centre to the falls.

IRIS 'HARMONY'

IRIS BUCHARICA ♀

'J.S. Dijt' is another small iris, which never fails to flower in the winter if planted in a sunny position. It has rich, purple flowers with orange on the falls.
'Katharine Hodgkin' ♀ This unusually coloured, small, bulbous iris was discovered in an English garden during the nineteenth century. It has distinctive, light-blue flowers with a mix of yellow and blue on the falls. A strong grower, this iris is invaluable for brightening up a gloomy late winter day, and is capable of withstanding the vagaries of winter. ▣◊ ❀❀❀

Also recommended: 'Joyce'

Xiphium iris ♀
I. latifolia, a medium iris from northern Spain, has violet flowers with yellow markings on the falls. ▣◊ ❀❀❀

GLADIOLUS 'MI MI'

Gladiolus

A widespread genus of cormous perennials from Africa and southern Europe. The Grandiflorus Group are half-hardy in frost-prone climates, so they are planted in spring and lifted in autumn, when the leaves begin to turn yellow. There are many selections of these tall plants with showy, open funnel-shaped flowers in midsummer. They can be planted in borders, or used in a more formal setting. 'Mi Mi' has deep pink flowers with white centres. ▣◊ ❀

G. communis subsp. *byzantinus* ♥ *p.37*
Also recommended: *G. tristis*

H

Hippeastrum

These bulbs are from South America, and can be stored at precise temperatures to flower at almost any time of the year, particularly in winter and spring. They form medium plants with large, trumpet-shaped flowers, varying from white to deep red, on a stout stem. In colder climates, they are ideal container plants, suitable for a sunny windowsill or conservatory. ▣◊❦

Hyacinthoides (Bluebell)

These vigorous bulbs pull themselves deeply into the soil with contractile roots. They grow well in most situations. *H. hispanica* (syn. *Scilla hispanica*, Spanish bluebell) is of medium height and tolerant of many garden positions but is excellent in a wilder setting, such as a wood or an orchard. The mid-blue flowers grow in a spire, with each one curving back at the tips. ▣◊ ❀❀❀
H. non-scripta (syn. *Scilla non-scripta*, English bluebell) is a vigorous, medium-height bulb, similar to *H. hispanica* but with backward curving, blue flowers held on one side of the flower spike only. The glossy leaves are dark green, and arch out from the base to frame the plant. If you do not want a large colony, remove the flowerheads before the seed is set. This bulb is also available in both white and pink forms. ▣◊ ❀❀❀

HIPPEASTRUM 'APPLE BLOSSOM'

HYACINTHOIDES NON-SCRIPTA

Hyacinthus (Hyacinth)

A familiar bulb with all the cultivars derived from the smaller and refined species *H. orientalis*. Dutch growers have been selecting these larger-flowered forms for over a hundred years, particularly for the forced flower market. *H. orientalis*, the ubiquitous hyacinth, is small in stature and available in a wide range of colours from white through pink to red, purple, and violet. Shades of yellow and apricot are also found. These are first-class bulbs for formal bedding in spring, or for containers, which can be prepared for early flowering. *H. orientalis* 'Anna Marie' ♥, has fragrant, tubular, bell-shaped pink flowers, held in a tight spike. This bulb is particularly good for forcing. *H. orientalis* 'Delft Blue' ♥ is a single, soft-blue form. *H. orientalis* 'White Pearl' is a slightly later, pure white, single-flowered selection. ▣◊ ❀❀❀
'Carnegie' *p.45*
'City of Haarlem' *p.45*
'L'Innocence' *p.45*
'Ostara' *p.45*

LILIUM (LILIES)

Lily hybrids are easier to cultivate than the species. However, the flowers of the species do have an allure and grace that is seldom found in the hybrids. Plant them in a deep hole incorporating organic matter. Lilies only need staking in windy sites, and most are ideal for pots with adequate root space.

Asiatic hybrids

'Connecticut King' is a tall, unscented lily with long-lasting, upward-facing, yellow flowers in summer. 'Enchantment' ♀ is prolific in the garden and good for cutting. In summer, this medium lily has unscented, upward-facing, orange flowers that curve back. 'Mont Blanc' is a medium, summer-flowering, vigorous lily, and has white, upward-facing, unscented flowers with brown spots. 'Red Night' (syn. 'Roter Cardinal') is a medium lily with upward-

LILIUM 'JOURNEY'S END'

facing, unscented flowers in early summer. It has light, black spots in the centre. ⧉◊ ✿✿✿

Oriental hybrids

'Casa Blanca' ♀ has pure white, bowl-shaped flowers, produced in summer in clusters on tall stems. They are scented and have contrasting dark orange anthers.
'Journey's End' is an unusual combination of pink and maroon, with white margins. This tall, broad and backward curving lily has very attractive, unscented flowers in late summer. ⧉◊ ✿✿✿

Trumpet hybrids

Golden Splendor Group lilies are tall trumpet lilies with dark, scented, yellow flowers veined with deep red. A summer-flowering, vigorous plant that will not need staking. ⧉◊ ✿✿✿

Species

L. martagon (Common turkscap lily) is tall with shiny, unpleasant smelling, pink-to-purple, turkscap flowers in early and midsummer. The dark green leaves grow in whorls. In the white form the leaves are apple-green. ⧉–⧉◊ ✿✿✿
L. regale ♀(Regal lily) is a tall Chinese lily. It has white, scented trumpet-shaped flowers stained brown-purple on the outside in midsummer. It needs full sun and rich soil for best results. ⧉◊ ✿✿✿
L. speciosum var. *rubrum* needs acid, moist soil. Its tall, dark stems have scented, pendulous, turkscap flowers of rich carmine marked with dark spots in late summer and early autumn. ⧉◊ ✿✿✿
L. superbum ♀ (American turkscap lily) is tall with unscented, orange-red, spotted flowers in autumn. The leaves grow in whorls. ⧉◊ ✿✿✿

LILIUM REGALE ♀

LILIUM 'RED NIGHT'

I

Ipheion

A small genus of bulbs from the eastern side of South America. They are related to onions and give off a familiar smell when the leaves are crushed, but the flowers, produced in spring, are often honey-scented.

I. uniflorum 'Wisley Blue' ♀ is nearly fully hardy and well worth trying in colder gardens. Ipheion is small with light-blue, star-shaped flowers and dense, grass-like leaves. It multiplies quickly and is useful when planted between shrubs or at the edge of a rock garden.
⊡◊ ✤✤✤

L

Leucojum (Snowflake)

The snowflakes are rather neglected. The three species described here are easy to grow and quick to multiply.

L. aestivum 'Gravetye Giant' ♀ (Summer snowflake) is a medium-growing bulbous plant, with glossy green, strap-shaped leaves and stems with up to eight white, pendulous green-tipped bells. This bulb is excellent in full sun by a pond, or in partial shade in a border. It may need a little support if planted in an exposed position.
⊡◊ ✤✤✤

L. autumnale ♀ is a delicate-looking, but hardy, small plant suitable for a raised bed or rock garden. The 1cm (½in) bell-shaped flowers are among the first flowers of autumn. They start to appear

Leucojum aestivum 'Gravetye Giant'

in late summer, and are soon followed by the grass-like leaves. ⊡◊ ✤✤✤

L. vernum ♀ (Spring snowflake) A small but robust plant with quite short strap-shaped leaves which are produced with the flowers in early spring. These flowers are open and bell-shaped, and are white with green or yellow tips. Spring snowflakes provide a taller growing alternative to snowdrops. ⊡◊ ✤✤✤

M

Muscari (Grape hyacinth)

Grape hyacinths are a group of easily cultivated bulbs, generally producing blue or white flowers in spring. They are well suited to almost all gardens and will soon spread to colonize an area.

M. armeniacum ♀ is a vigorous, small plant with spikes of bright-blue, bell-like flowers with constricted white mouths appearing in spring. The thin, strap-shaped leaves are produced

Muscari armeniacum ♀

in autumn. This bulb is ideal for planting in wild or isolated parts of the garden, where its spreading habit may be an asset. ⊡◊ ✤✤✤

M. azureum ♀, syn. *Hyacinthus azureus,* is a small bulb with upright, greyish leaves and is well suited to rock gardens, where the bright-blue flowers can be appreciated. It may seed prolifically, so it is good for producing drifts of colour in borders in spring. ⊡◊ ✤✤✤

M. latifolium is a small, spring-flowering plant with just one or two broader leaves and a bi-coloured spike of violet-black, fertile florets at the base and pale blue infertile florets above. Slower growing than most grape hyacinths and not as vigorous as some.
⊡◊ ✤✤✤

M. macrocarpum is still small in stature but has large, yellow, highly fragrant flowers in spring. This bulb needs a hot, dry, well-drained position to grow well and is ideally suited to a raised bed. ⊡◊ ✤✤

NARCISSUS (DAFFODILS)

The range of daffodils on offer is vast. The shape and colour of each cultivar is clear from the illustrations in catalogues and garden centres. Equally important, however, is the height – some large-flowered daffodils need plenty of space and require careful placing. The varieties listed here are mostly medium in stature, and easily cultivated. Buy daffodils as soon as they go on sale, because the roots will begin to grow in late summer.

Daffodils for borders
'Cheerfulness' ♀ has a sweetly scented, double white flower, with creamy-yellow petals forming the trumpet. It is a medium height bulb and has mid-season flowers.
'Dove Wings' ♀ has white, swept-back outer petals and a lemon-yellow trumpet. This is a small but sturdy and free-flowering bulb.

NARCISSUS 'CHEERFULNESS' ♀

'February Gold' ♀ often begins flowering in very early spring. It has a stunning all gold-coloured, medium flower, with a darker trumpet.
'Irene Copeland' has a double flower with white outer petals and a bright yellow double trumpet. It grows to medium height and flowers in mid-spring.
'Jack Snipe' ♀ is a small plant with white outer petals and a lemon-yellow trumpet. It flowers well and bulks up very quickly.
'Jetfire' is also small and has a good contrast between its yellow outer petals and bright orange trumpet. At first the trumpet is quite pale in colour but soon darkens with time.
'Minnow' ♀ is a small, multi-headed, scented narcissus with pale yellow trumpets surrounded by cream outer petals. This daffodil is best grown in a large container or a raised bed.
'Mount Hood' ♀ is a medium-height daffodil with a cream trumpet and whiter outer petals. It has a mid-spring flower of good substance.
'Pipit' is a scented, medium-height daffodil, with two to three lemon flowers per stem.
'Tête-à-Tête' ♀ is small but vigorous, with up to three flowers per stem. It has yellow outer petals, and a golden trumpet.
'Thalia' has a neat, creamy-white flower with a small, open trumpet of medium

NARCISSUS 'TÊTE-À-TÊTE'

height. A prolific plant, it will flower regularly without being lifted.
▨◊ ✤✤✤

Daffodils for forcing
N. Papyraceus has a white form available in autumn, sold as **'Paper White'** to flower in midwinter. Of medium height, it produces small, fragrant, white flowers. It does well in mild gardens.
▨◊ ✤✤ (Also **'Jack Snipe'**, **'Minnow'** and **'Tête-à-Tête'**)

Daffodils for naturalizing
N. poeticus var. *recurvus* ♀ (Old pheasant's eye) This medium-height daffodil has white outer petals and small red-rimmed, yellow cups.
N. pseudonarcissus (syn. *N. lobularis*, Lent lily, Wild daffodil) This is a small but willing naturalizer from Europe. It is a classic daffodil, with nodding yellow trumpets and cream outer petals.
▨◊ ✤✤✤ (Also **'February Gold'**)

NERINE BOWDENII ♀

N

Nerine

A South African genus of small to medium bulbs that flowers in autumn in the Northern hemisphere. Nerines are dormant during the dry summer, flowering in autumn with the leaves emerging afterwards. There are many hybrids that are excellent for conservatories or containers. Where the climate is mild, species thrive in sheltered spots. *N. bowdenii* ♀ is under-rated for the autumn, being small in stature but with large clusters of lily-like, pink flowers on stout stems. The bulbs should be planted shallowly on the sunny side of a wall, where they will flower year after year with very little attention. They are excellent cut flowers. ⊡◊ ❀❀❀

O

Ornithogalum (Star-of-Bethlehem)

A large genus with a few spring-flowering, hardy representatives that are easy to grow in the open.

O. nutans ♀ A mid-spring flowering, small bulb with truly silvery-white pendent, bell-shaped flowers held in a one-sided spike. These are held above slightly succulent leaves with a central silver stripe. A quietly attractive plant to place close to the path or border's edge, so it can be viewed at close quarters.

O. umbellatum (Star-of-Bethlehem) A tough, small plant, ideal for areas where little else will grow, such as the base of hedges or tight against a building. In good growing conditions, it may increase too rapidly. The starry, white flowers have a green stripe externally and form a dense cluster. ⊡–◧◊ ❀❀❀

O. pyrenaicum p.37
Also recommended:
O. narbonense

Oxalis (Shamrock, Sorrel)

A huge genus of very varied plants, all with the typical five-petalled flowers, which are twisted in the bud stage.

OXALIS ADENOPHYLLA ♀

O. adenophylla ♀ is a very small bulb from South America, which will grow well in a rock garden or large container. It has a wide, funnel-shaped, single, dark pink flower with a paler centre produced in late spring. ⊡◊ ❀❀❀

P

Puschkinia

A small, spring-flowering genus from western Asia, needing a well-drained site. *P. scilloides* is a small bulb with two upright leaves and tight heads of pale blue, open, bell-shaped flowers with a darker blue line down the centre of each petal. This is a very adaptable plant that will grow in full sun or partial shade. ⊡–◧◊ ❀❀❀

S

Scilla

This is a good bulb for bringing a true blue to the garden in early spring.

SCILLA BIFOLIA ♀

S. *bifolia* ♀ is a very small bulb that will brighten up any part of the garden in early spring with its bluish, starry flowers. The dark green leaves are sparse and have a hooked tip. There are also white and pink forms. ▣◊ ❀❀❀

S. *peruviana* Despite the name, this bulb hails from the western Mediterranean. It is small, and unusual in that it is virtually evergreen – its many tapering leaves are produced in the autumn, long before it blooms in early summer in a many-flowered, conical, violet-blue or white flowerhead. ▣◊ ❀❀

S. *siberica* 'Spring Beauty', syn. 'Atrocoerulea', is a little taller than S. *bifolia* and has deep blue, more pendent flowers in early spring. It looks very effective when planted around deciduous shrubs or in conjunction with white or red flowers. ▣◊ ❀❀❀

Sternbergia

(Autumn daffodil)
This bulb provides a welcome and stunning contrast to the predominantly pink flowers of other autumnal bulbs.

S. *lutea* is a small plant for a sunny spot. In autumn, it has bright yellow, goblet-shaped flowers, surrounded by dark green, narrow, strap-shaped leaves. This is a tough little plant, and it will continue to flower well into winter if the weather is mild. ▣◊ ❀❀❀

S. *sicula* is a small bulb that has bright, butter-yellow flowers. It demands a hot, sunny spot, where the thin, dark green leaves contrast well with the yellow goblet-shaped flowers. ▣◊ ❀❀

TULIPA (TULIPS)

This popular genus of perennial, spring-flowering bulbs revels in sunny, warm conditions during the summer. It may be necessary to lift the bulbs in late spring and replant them in the autumn, depending on the conditions in your garden. There are hundreds of cultivars to choose from. ▣◊ ❀❀❀

Bowl-shaped flowers
T. linifolia Batalinii Group ♀ These are small to medium, early-flowering tulips that come in red, yellow, apricot, and bronze. They are very easy to grow if planted in a well-drained spot in a cold garden.

T. praestans 'Fusilier' ♀ is a barely medium-height tulip that is particularly easily grown and very reliable. It has several vibrant, red flowers, on each stem.

TULIPA LINIFOLIA

'Red Riding Hood' ♀ is a small tulip, which has attractive green leaves marked with dark maroon patches. The outside of the flower is red, but inside it is scarlet with a black base.

Single cup-shaped flowers
'Attila' is of medium height with a single, pink-violet flower. It grows well in pots and can be planted closely or with annuals.
'Queen of Night' is a medium tulip that flowers later in the season, with very dark maroon flowers and plain green leaves. It is very effective grown alongside white flowers.

Goblet-shaped flowers
'Queen of Sheba' ♀ is a medium-height, late-flowering tulip, with red flowers edged with orange.

Also recommended:
T. sprengeri ♀

TULIPA 'QUEEN OF SHEBA' ♀

INDEX

Page numbers in *italics* indicate illustrations.

A, B

Allium 9, 14, *14*, 28, *30*, 31, *32*, 56, 61, 65
  A. cernuum 19, 36, 37, 65
  A. cristophii 9, 13, 15, 31, *36*, 37, 65
  A. 'Hidcote' 65
  A. hollandicum 13, 14, 15, 31, 36, 37, 42, 65
    'Purple Sensation' 14, 15
  A. insubricum 37
  A. moly 19, 36, 46, 65, *65*
  A. oreophilum 37
  A. rosenbachianum 14
  A. schubertii 14, 15
  A. ursinum 22
Amaryllis 10, 12, 17, 65
  A. belladonna 10, 38, *39*, 65
Anemone *12*, 26, 66
  A. blanda 8, *8*, 42, 43, 66
  A. coronaria 43, 47, 66, *66*
  A. × *fulgens* 26, 66
  A. nemorosa 25, 51, 57, 66
  A. pavonina 9, 26, 42
autumn 10, 17, 29, 38–39, 63
basal rot 62
Begonia *20*, 19, 63, 66
bluebell, *see Hyacinthoides*
bulb blindness 62
bulb planter 51, *51*, 52
buying bulbs 49, 62, 63

C

calendar 63
Camassia 9, 28, 52, 54, 56, 66
  C. cusickii 9, 20, 29, 66
  C. leichtlinii 20, 66, *66*
    'Semiplena' 9, 47, 66
Canna 7, 17, 26, 31, 46, 47, 66
  'Assaut' *20*, 26, *31*, 66, *66*
  'King Midas' 26, 66
Cardiocrinum giganteum 9, 15, *15*, 17, 28, 31, 37, 42, 66–67, *67*

care 54–55, 59
Chionodoxa 8, 19, 67
  C. luciliae 8, 34, 35, 67
Colchicum 10, *11*, 17, 25, 56, 67
  C. byzantinum 10, 67
  C. 'Pink Goblet' 39
  C. speciosum 'Album' 10, 29, 38, 47, 67, *67*
  C. tenorei 19, 67
  C. 'Waterlily' 10, 38, *38*, 47, 67
colour *6*, 26–29
containers 18–21, 46–47, 63
  planting in 53
corms 7, 57
Corydalis 16, 56, 67
  C. malkensis 40, 42, 43, 67
  C. solida 43, 67
Crinum × *powellii* 36, 37, 67, *67*
Crocosmia 16, *16*, 26, *27*, 31, 68
  C. × *crocosmiiflora* 'Dusky Maiden' 13, 37, 68
    'Emily McKenzie' 26, 68
    'Gerbe d'Or' 46, 68
    'Jackanapes' 46, *47*, 68
    'Star of the East' 13, 26, 68, *68*
  C. 'Lucifer' 37, 68
Crocus 7, 16, 19, 23, 25, 28, 51, 57, 68
  autumn 10, 25, 38, 39, 68
  C. ancyrensis 68
  C. chrysanthus 'Blue Pearl' 34, 35, 68
    'Cream Beauty' 68
    'Ladykiller' 68
  C. kotschyanus 39
  C. × *luteus* 'Golden Yellow' 68
  C. medius 25, 68
  C. ochroleucus 25, 39, 68
  C. sieberi 'Albus' 29, 40, 68
    'Hubert Edelsten' 68, *68*
    'Violet Queen' 40
  C. speciosus 'Oxonian' 10, *29*, 38, 39, 68

  C. tommasinianus 19, 68
    'Ruby Giant' 19, 68, *68*
Crown Imperial, *see Fritillaria imperialis*
cut flowers 12–13, 23
Cyclamen 7, 13, 16, 19, 23, 61, 63, 68–69
  C. cilicium 39, 69
  C. coum 11, *11*, 19, 25, 28, 30, 41, *41*, 69
  C. hederifolium 7, 10, 16, 25, 29, 30, 38, 39, 69
  C. persicum 69
  C. repandum 69
Cyrtanthus elatus 69

D, E

daffodil, *see Narcissus*
Dahlia 7, 9, 10, 13, 19, *19*, 54, 61, 62, 63, 69
  'Bishop of Llandaff' 16, 26, 69
  'Charlie Two' 69
  'Fascination' 19, 69, *69*
  'Glorie van Heemstede' 69
  'Grenidor Pastelle' 69
  'Mi Wong' 69
  Unwins Dwarf Group 46, 69
dividing bulbs 60, 61, *61*, 63
dog's-tooth violet, *see Erythronium*
Eranthis 11, 25, 52, 60, 61, 69
  E. hyemalis 40, 41, 69, *69*
Erythronium 16, 28, 30, 57, 70
  E. californicum 17, 70
  E. dens-canis 17, 35, 70
  E. 'Pagoda' 34, 35, 70
  E. revolutum 17, 42, 43, 70
Eucomis bicolor 20, 38, 39, 70, *70*
  E. pole-evansii 39, 70

F, G

fertilizer 50, 55, 63
floristry 11–13
foliage 16–17, 30–31
  tidying 56, 63

forcing 58–59, 63, 75
form and structure 30–31
formal beds 44 –45
Fritillaria 14, 15, 16, 23,
31, 51, 63, 70
F. imperialis 17, *17*, 23,
31, 35, *42*, 43, 44, 70
'Rubra' 45, 70
'The Premier' 45, 70
F. meleagris 25, 28, 34, 35,
70, *70*
F. pallidiflora 18, 28
F. persica 34, 35
'Adiyaman' 43, 70
Galanthus 11, 13, 19, 22, 25,
28, 49, 52, 56, 61, 63,
70–71
G. elwesii 40, 42, 70
G. 'Magnet' 40
G. nivalis 11, 19, 25, 40,
42, 43, 71
G. plicatus 29, 40, 71
subsp. *byzantinus* 35, 41,
70
Galtonia 9, 21, 28, 71
G. candicans 9, 29, 37, 46,
47, 71, *71*
garden design 33
giant lily, *see Cardiocrinum*
Gladiolus 9, 12, 16, 20, 54,
54, 57, 63, 72
G. communis subsp.
byzantinus 37, 72
G. 'Mi Mi' 72, *72*
G. tristis 23, 72
Grandiflorus Group 13, 72
glory of the snow, *see*
Chionodoxa
golden garlic, *see Allium moly*
grape hyacinth, *see Muscari*

H, I
Hippeastrum 11, 40, 59, 72, *72*
Hyacinthoides 24, 29, 48, 51, 72
H. hispanica 25, 72
H. non-scripta 23, 25, 72, *72*
Hyacinthus 11, 13, 23, *23*,
29, 54, 58, 59, 72
H. 'L'Innocence' 58, 72
H. orientalis 19, 23, 45, 72
H. 'Ostara' 58, 72

"in the green" 52, 56
Ipheion uniflorum 'Wisley
Blue' 8, 42, 43, 74
Iris 71
I. bucharica 17, 71, *71*
I. 'Harmony' 19, 35, 71, *71*
I. 'J.S. Dijt' 35, 71
I. 'Joyce' 23, 71
I. 'Katharine Hodgkin' 19,
43, 43, 71
I. latifolia 71

L
layered border 42–43
Leucojum 25, 28, 49, 52, 63,
74
L. aestivum 'Gravetye
Giant' 13, 74, *74*
L. autumnale 74
L. vernum 25, *40*, 41, 42, 74
lifting bulbs 54, 56, 63
Lilium 7, 9, 12, 13, 14, 16–17,
19, 21, *21*, 22, 25, 28,
31, 54, *54*, 61, 63, 73
Golden Splendor Group 47,
73
L. 'Casa Blanca' 73
L. 'Connecticut King' 73
L. 'Enchantment' 73
L. formosanum 39
L. 'Journey's End' 73, *73*
L. 'Marie North' 9
L. martagon 9, 17, 31, 37,
42, 73
L. 'Mont Blanc' 73
L. pomponium 26
L. pumilium 26
L. pyrenaicum 33
L. 'Red Night' 37, 73, *73*
L. regale 37, 73, *73*
L. speciosum 10, 17, 20
var. *rubrum* 20, 39, 47, 73
L. superbum 17, 20, 31, 73

M, N
montbretia, *see Crocosmia*
moving bulbs 56, *56*, 57, 63
mulching 55, *55*, 63
Muscari 6, 19, 23, 25, 28, *28*,
31, 74

M. armeniacum 42, 45, 74,
74
M. azureum 34, 35, 42, 43,
74
M. latifolium 35, 74
M. macrocarpum 23, 74
Narcissus 7, 8, 11, 13, *13*, 16,
19, 25, *25*, 28, 31, 54,
56, 57, 58, 61, 63, 75
N. 'Cheerfulness' 8, 75, *75*
N. 'Dove Wings' 8, 75
N. 'February Gold' 8, 35, 75
N. 'Irene Copeland' 8, 75
N. 'Jack Snipe' 8, *8*, 35, 75
N. 'Jetfire' 8, 35, 75
N. jonquilla 22
N. 'Minnow' 8, 75
N. 'Mount Hood' 8, 75
N. 'Paper White' 58, 75
N. 'Pipit' 23, 75
N. poeticus var. *recurvus* 75
N. pseudonarcissus 24, 75
N. 'Rijnveld's Early
Sensation' 40
N. 'Tête-à-Tête' 42, 45, 75,
75
N. 'Thalia' 8, 29, 35, 75
narcissus bulb fly 62, 63
naturalizing bulbs 24–25, 51,
56, 75
Nerine 10, 12, 17, 61, 76
N. bowdenii 10, 13, 38,
39, 47, 76, *76*
N. undulata 19

O–P
Orchis morio 25
Ornithogalum 25, 28, 76
O. narbonense 29, 76
O. nutans 19, 29, 34, 35,
43, 76
O. pyrenaicum 37, 76
O. umbellatum 19, 76
Oxalis adenophylla 36, 76, *76*
pests 62, 63
planting 52–53, 63
in containers 53, 58
in grass 24, 51, *51*
planting depths 51, *51*
plants to grow with bulbs 32,
33, 34–47

preparing soil 50, *50*, 52, 63
problems 62
propagation 60–61
Puschkinia scilloides 28, 43, 76

R–S
rhizomes 7
rot, storage 62
scent 22–23
Scilla 8, 25, 28, 61, 76–77
  S. bifolia 35, 42, 43, *76*, 77
  S. peruviana 77
  S. siberica 'Spring Beauty' 8, 77
seasonal bulbs 7, 8-11, 19
seedheads 14–15, *60*
seeds 60, *60*, 63
soil, improving 50
snowdrop, *see Galanthus*
snowflake, *see Leucojum*
spring 8, 34–35, 63

staking 54, 63
star-of-Bethlehem, *see Ornithogalum*
Sternbergia 13, 77
  S. lutea 10, 38, 39, 77
  S. sicula 77
storing bulbs 57, 62, 63
summer 9, 28, 36–37, 63
sunken containers 20–21, 53
supports 54, 63

T
tubers 7, *53*, 57, 60, 62
Tulipa 6, 8, 13, *13*, 14, 15, 16, *18*, 20, *21*, 23, 25, 26, 51, 57, 77
  T. 'Attila' 77
  T. 'Golden Apeldoorn' 45
  T. kaufmanniana 17, *64*
  T. kolpakowskiana 17
  T. linifolia 8, 26, 43, 47, 77

T. praestans 'Fusilier' 8, 26, 35, 42, 77
  'Unicum' 17
  T. 'Purissima' 8, 29, 44, 45
  T. 'Queen of Night' 34, 35, 45, 77
  T. 'Queen of Sheba' 35, *44*, 44, 77, *77*
  T. 'Red Riding Hood' 26, 31, 77
  T. sprengeri 77
  T. 'White Triumphator' 8, 45

W
water, growing in 59
winter 11, 28, 40–41, 63
winter aconite, *see Eranthis*
wood anemone, *see Anemone nemorosa* 7
woodland 24, 25, *25*

ACKNOWLEDGMENTS

Picture research Anna Grapes
  Mariana Sonnenberg
Picture librarians Richard Dabb
  Romaine Werblow

Planting plan illustrations Anne Winterbotham
Additional illustration Sharon Moore

Index Chris Bernstein

Dorling Kindersley would like to thank:
All staff at the RHS, in particular Susanne Mitchell, Karen Wilson and Barbara Haynes at Vincent Square. Thanks also to Joanna Chisholm for editorial assistance.

Studio Cactus would like to thank:
Susi Bailey, Alison Bolus, Sue Gordon, and Kate Hayward for editorial assistance; Lesley Malkin for proofreading; Alison Donovan, Claire Pegrum, Ann Thompson, and Laura Watson for design assistance. Thanks also to Mr and Mrs Lunn and Mr and Mrs Trown for the use of their gardens.

The Royal Horticultural Society
To learn more about the work of the Society, visit the RHS on the internet at **www.rhs.org.uk**. Information offered includes plant news, horticultural events around the country, *RHS Plant Finder*, a garden finder, international plant registers, results of plant trials, a gardening calendar and monthly topics of interest, publications and membership details.

Photography
The publisher would also like to thank the following for their kind permission to reproduce their photographs:
(key: t=top, c=centre, b=below, l=left, r=right)
Sue Atkinson: 3
Jonathan Buckley: 23tl.
Jacqui Hurst: 64
Rod Leeds: 9tl, 11cr, 33bl.
Harry Smith Collection: 15bl.